James E. (James Edward) McGee

Sketches of Irish Soldiers in Every Land

James E. (James Edward) McGee

Sketches of Irish Soldiers in Every Land

ISBN/EAN: 9783337126582

Printed in Europe, USA, Canada, Australia, Japan

Cover: Foto ©ninafisch / pixelio.de

More available books at **www.hansebooks.com**

SKETCHES

OF

IRISH SOLDIERS

IN

EVERY LAND.

BY

COLONEL JAMES E. McGEE.

NEW YORK:
J. A. McGEE, Publisher,
7 Barclay St.
1873.

Stereotyped at the New York Catholic Protectory, West Chester, N. Y.

PRINTERS,
108 TO 114 WOOSTER STREET, N. Y.

TO THE MEMORY

OF

THE FEARLESS IRISHMEN

WHO FOUGHT AND FELL, DURING THE LATE

WAR,

IN DEFENCE OF

THE LIBERTY AND INTEGRITY

OF THEIR

ADOPTED COUNTRY,

THIS LITTLE VOLUME IS FONDLY AND

PROUDLY DEDICATED.

PREFACE.

In presenting to the public the following sketches, I am fully aware that I have left out many names of distinguished Irishmen, and omitted or merely glanced at several incidents, historical and biographical, which, if fully related, would redound to the national credit of my chivalrous countrymen in every part of the world. These omissions have not been intentional, but necessary.

Within the limits assigned to this book, it was impossible to find place for even the mention of the names of the myriad of heroic Irish soldiers who, during the seventeenth century, battled for religious freedom and independence at home, or who, in the eighteenth, filled the continent of Europe, the Indies, east and west, and our own colonies, with the fame of their bravery and daring. The incidents connected with their brilliant and varied careers, are also so numerous, and so amplified by contemporary writers, that it would require an ordinary lifetime to arrange them with any thing like system, and to record them with a proper degree of clearness and fidelity.

When we consider that, from the surrender of Limerick till the era of the French Revolution, three-quarters of a million of adults of Irish birth served in the armies and navies of Europe alone; that they were to be found fighting under every flag on the continent, according as their inclination or family ties led them to the choice of a home; that they were, even under the same government, divided into various brigades, regiments, parts of regiments, and independent commands; that their officers, forced from their native soil by persecuting and proscriptive laws, were men whose fortunes lay in their swords, and whose advancement depended neither on court favor nor social influence, but on their individual capacity and conduct in actual warfare,—we can form some estimate of what a mass of facts, dates, episodes, and anecdotes, an author would have to collate and examine, who aimed at publishing all the gallant deeds performed by Irishmen even for two or three generations.

My object was less ambitious; for I desired only to portray a few of these noble actions,—to cull, as it were, some flowers from the immortal garlands with which modern history has enwreathed the brow of Irish valor, and, by presenting them in a well-assorted bouquet, to show to the world, in miniature form, what grateful tributes have been offered to the exiled and long-suffering children of the land in which I had the honor of being born.

While selecting prominent characters, and incidentally touching on the relation of important battles, I have endeavored also to preserve as much as possible a chronological sequence, so that those who have neither leisure nor inclination to study the history of the last three centuries, as it elucidates the condition and afflictions of Ireland, may incidentally gain some notion of the motives, aims, and innate strength of her people, while amusing themselves with the moving accounts of practical warfare.

It is almost unnecessary to say that the present collection of evidences of Irish prowess and skill on many a well-fought field, is not intended to demonstrate them in the past or present to the general public; for, whatever other quality may be refused to that people, courage has never been denied them. England herself, who, like the ancient Romans, is not satisfied with subduing a weaker nation, but always seeks to justify her wrong by destroying in the minds of others the character of its people, cannot deny them the attribute of courage. But she does all in her power, all that her ingenuity can suggest, and her malice propagate, to lessen its grand moral effect. Were we to believe her officials, her scribes and caricaturists, the Irish, even at their best, are good only at a "shindy," a wild half-intoxicated foray, or a reckless, headlong charge. That, in fact, our courage is that of the wild animal which shuts its eyes and rushes on the foe, not the sterling bravery that can patiently endure suffering and fatigue, coolly advance and steadily retire, equally patient and formidable in defeat or victory; and this in despite of the repeated proofs afforded by her own military annals; that, in fact, we are fit only to be led, and not to be leaders.

Now nothing can be more fallacious or unjust than this estimate of Irish military character, sought to be impressed upon the belief of other nations by our enemy. Keeping in view the force of class influence and political preference, which have in all countries exercised such a potent influence in the promotion of army officers, as well as the effect of national prejudices and the advantages which a knowledge of the vernacular justly affords the native-born, we are surprised to find how numerous were the general officers of Irish birth, not to speak of those of Irish extraction, whose names are to be found on the muster-rolls of every army in Europe, within the space of one hundred and fifty years. From Lacy in Russia, to Field-Marshal Nugent in Austria, who but recently died, Irish officers, relying solely on their intrinsic merits, their bravery, fidelity, and genius, have been among the most trusted and distinguished commanders in every country in Europe, from the time that all hope of rescuing their country from the thraldom of England by the strong arm had been abandoned by her wisest and bravest sons.

It is true that in later times the direction of the tide of Irish emigration, as well as the character of the emigrants, has been changed. America, not Europe, is now opening her hospitable bosom to receive and welcome the oppressed; not as dashing, hot-blooded, and educated soldiers to fight her battles, but as humble, loyal, yet still stalwart citizens, to till her inexhaustible fields and level her interminable forests. But it is well that our adopted country should know—if the events of the late civil war have not convinced her—that the pluck and hardihood that were displayed so prominently on the battle-fields of France and Spain, Italy and Germany, by the Irishmen of past generations, are as strong and vigorous in their descendants of to-day, and as ready to be displayed in the cause of the country that gives them what they are yet denied at home,—civil and religious freedom.

I may be allowed to add that, in compiling these sketches, I have aimed more at accuracy of description than at originality, and that I have been indebted to the works of several authors, to whom I have endeavored to give full credit in the text or notes, and, amongst others, to John Cornelius O'Callaghan, whose *History of the Irish Brigades in the Service of France* is a work of rare industry and research, and an inexhaustible mine of information on that particular subject.

J. E. M.

NEW YORK, *May*, 1873.

CONTENTS.

	PAGE
HUGH O'NEILL. — Battle of the Yellow Ford	1
OWEN ROE O'NEILL. — Battle of Benburb	12
A FIGHTING BISHOP. — The Confederation of Kilkenny	19
PATRICK SARSFIELD. — Defence of Limerick	57
SERGEANT COSTUME. — The Siege of Athlone	76
UNDRESS UNIFORM. — The Surprise of Cremona	81
CAPTAIN JAMES CANTILLON. — Battle of Malplaquet	93
FIELD MARSHAL COUNT PETER LACY. — His Campaigns as Commander of the Russian forces	96
LIEUTENANT-GENERAL DANIEL O'MAHONY. — The Wars of the Spanish Succession	124
CHEVALIER WOGAN. — Stealing a Princess	138
AN OLD-FASHIONED DUEL. — Swords for Four; Coffee for Two	148
LORD CLARE. — Battle of Fontenoy	152
CAPTAIN CAREW. — Implicit Obedience	160
MAJOR-GENERAL RICHARD MONTGOMERY. — The Invasion of Canada	162

CONTENTS.

PAGE

JOHN SULLIVAN. — How he seized an opportunity and some cannon 173
MAD ANTHONY WAYNE. — Capture of Stony Point . 176
GENERAL JOHN STARK. — Battle of Bennington . 180
GENERAL EDWARD HAND. — How a Doctor killed his enemies instead of his patients . . . 185
COLONEL FITZGERALD. — Battle of Princeton, N. J. 189
COMMODORE JOHN BARRY. — Organization of the American Navy 193
THE MEN OF '98. — The Wexford Insurrection . 203
GENERAL COUNT O'CONNELL. — Last days of the Irish Brigade in France 252
COUNT O'SHEA. — Sweet Revenge 258
CAPTAIN O'REILLY. — A Brigade Officer of the Old School 261
DANIEL O'CONNELL. — His duel with D'Esterre . 266
ADVENTURES BY FLOOD AND FIELD. — A Sailor on Shore 289
THE 88TH RANGERS. — "Connaught Robbers" . 299
GENERAL THOMAS W. SWEENY. — Battles of Cerro Gordo and Shiloh 303
GENERAL MICHAEL CORCORAN. — The 69th at Bull Run 311
WHO WON THE "BRITISH" VICTORIES. — Battles by Land and Sea 326

IRISH SOLDIERS.

HUGH O'NEILL.

BATTLE OF THE YELLOW FORD.

HUGH, or, as he is more properly called in the Gælic vernacular, AODHA O'NEILL, was of a race the most distinguished in the annals of any country for hereditary military prowess and deeds of valor. For at least fifteen hundred years he could trace back his ancestors in an unbroken line, every one of whom was a soldier and a prince. Like his progenitors, as far as we have a description of their *personnel*, he was tall, muscular, and handsome, well skilled in the art of warfare, as then known, and of undaunted courage. To these noble qualities he, however, unlike most of them, added that of profound dissimulation, and a conscience not over scrupulous as to means when an end was to be gained. In early life he had served as an ensign in the French army, and afterwards in a higher grade in that of England. As Earl of Tyrone, an English title conferred on and accepted by one of his immediate predecessors, he was much at Elizabeth's court, and even, it is said, a favorite of that fickle and infamous woman; and it was in the companionship of such men as Cecil and Monteagle that he learned those arts of trickery and deception which he afterwards practised against them with such marked effect. The difference between them and him was, that they used their treachery to persecute and harass their countrymen and even to betray their country, while he found it the most effective weapon he could use against the deceitful enemies of his race and nation.

When he retired from the English service he went to Ulster and took up his residence at the ancestral mansion, where he spent a long time secretly preparing for a war on the palesmen. His arrangements were on a very extensive scale, his plans exhibited great comprehensiveness, and his design evidently was to drive the English out of Ireland and to become king of the whole country. This result, so much to have been desired, at one period of his subsequent career, seemed to friends and foes alike to be not only possible, but very probable indeed.

In 1595, O'Neill having his scheme completed, as far as he could with his limited means, took occasion to provoke a quarrel with the English authorities in Ireland, by ignominiously expelling a sheriff whom they had sent into his country. He was accused of this crime by his brother-in-law, Sir Henry Bagnal, who entertained for him the most implacable hatred; and for his wide domain, in case of confiscation, a proportionate affection. Tyrone contented himself with a protestation of innocence, but wisely withdrew to his own fastnesses and to the protection of his castles. Foiled in their attempt on his person, Sir John Norris, a brave and experienced commander, was sent against him with a considerable body of troops to bring him to terms, but "*the* O'Neill," the title he now reassumed, though with fewer numbers and without any regular equipments or cannon, so hung on his flanks and annoyed his foraging parties, that the English general was forced to abandon, for that season at least, the main enterprise, and retreat on Newry. "Norris," says O'Connor, "next proceeded to raise the siege of Monaghan invested by the insurgents. A rivulet separated the armies, each of which seemed to dread the event of a battle. A sharp encounter ensued in which Norris had three horses killed under him, and he and his brother were forced by their wounds to retire from the heat of the conflict. Segrave, an English officer, at the head of a body of cavalry made a furious assault on O'Neill's quarters; Tyrone encountered him in single combat. Their lances being shivered on each other's cuirass, the vigorous arm of O'Neill wielding a ponderous sword, clove down his adversary. Norris sounded a retreat, and Monaghan surrendered to the victorious army."

This success was but the prelude to a much greater victory, the most glorious and complete that has ever been won by Irishmen on their own soil, since that of Clontarf, in the early part of the eleventh century. This battle is known to the people of the neighborhood to this day as that of *Beal-an-atha-buidhe* (the Yellow Ford), on the river Blackwater, and took place on the 10th of August, 1595.

The night previous Sir Henry Bagnal occupied Armagh with his army, well equipped, officered, supplied with artillery, ammunition, and stores, and anticipating an easy conquest. O'Neill on his side, anticipating an attack, took up a strong position near the Ford, and to compensate for his deficiency in numbers and ordnance, threw up breastworks, partially to protect his front and flanks, with pits in advance containing sharp-pointed stakes, covered slightly with grass and herbs, after the manner of

Bruce at Bannockburn. At daylight on that eventful day, the English army marched out of Armagh to attack the Irish behind their works. The head of the column was led by Bagnal in person, who, though an arrant coward, felt such undying enmity towards Tyrone and was so confident of an easy victory, that he forgot all prudence and even his natural timidity. His centre was commanded by Crosby and Wingfield, two excellent officers, and his rear division by Cuin and Billing. Brooke, Montacute, and Fleming's cavalry protected his flanks. The first opposition which Bagnal met was from an enfilading fire of musketry from some Irish troops stationed in a piece of dense pine forest which lined either side of the road, some distance in advance of the main body. Those, however, after considerable loss to the enemy, were driven out of the woods and pressed back on the entrenchments, and the English without further interruption debouched into the open plain, and formed their order of battle within sight of their opponents.

The conflict now commenced in earnest. Bagnal's artillery being within short range, battered the slight earthworks of Tyrone into a shapeless mass; and his first division of infantry, supported by some light cavalry, made a desperate onslaught on the brave defenders. The cavalry, however, too late discovered the pitfalls that had been dug for them, and man and horse sunk down in them, irretrievably lost; those who were not disabled by the Irish musketeers being crushed to death by their own horses. The infantry, however, under cover of the incessant artillery fire advanced to the works, and even succeeded, at a great sacrifice of life, in capturing a portion of them. O'Neill, who never missed an opportunity to strike a deadly blow, saw that his time was now come; so, bringing up the main body of his forces, he ordered a general charge along the line, "horse, foot, and dragoons," and with one wild cheer the entire army precipitated itself on the foe. Only those who have seen an Irish charge can appreciate the effect of such a movement. The shock was irresistible. The infantry were scattered like chaff before a whirlwind, and the horsemen went down before the heavy swords and sharp pikes of the Celts, like grass before the scythe. The resistance at first was stubborn, such as might have been expected from veterans who had long seen service in the Low Countries as well as in Ireland; but having lost their best officers, and fearing to be utterly annihilated, they at length broke and fled in dismay, pursued to the very gates of Armagh by the victorious Irish.

O'Neill of course headed this charge, and, sword in hand, to use the classic language of this day, "went for" his ill-conditioned brother-in-law, who, had they met, would undoubtedly have shared the fate of Colonel Segrave, but he had already paid the penalty of his temerity; for, some time previously, upon raising his visor to inhale the fresh air, he was shot in the face by an unknown marksman, and fell lifeless from his saddle. Twenty-two superior officers, not counting lieutenants and ensigns, and twenty-five hundred men were killed in the battle and pursuit on the side of the enemy, while the Irish only lost two hundred, and three times that amount wounded. All the cannon, stores, horses, and standards of the English fell into the hands of the victors, besides a large supply of clothing and provisions, of which they stood in great need.

The effect of this grand success was electrical throughout Ireland. In Connaught, every man who could bear arms hastened to join O'Neill, and the Irish of the south prepared to follow their example. The English "authorities" in Dublin began to realize the doubtful nature of their tenure of office; and, had the promised supplies from Spain arrived in time, there can be no doubt that English power in Ireland would have been for ever destroyed.

* * * * *

"This man, Bagnal, hated Tyrone with implacable animosity; and, indeed, the earl reciprocated—nay, branded him in public and private as a coward who shrank from the ordeal of single combat."

"Single combat!" interrupted Father Purcell, "surely Tyrone was not justified in accepting or proposing such!"

"Have you not read," replied the provincial, "how Wenceslaus, the canonized duke of Bohemia, offered to enter the lists and fight his mortal enemy, Radislaus?"

"Yes," answered Purcell; "but the legend tells how an angel armed Wenceslaus in celestial panoply, and forbade his adversary to unsheathe the sword. Be that as it may," continued the provincial, "Bagnal refused to encounter Tyrone, when the latter proposed to meet him—nay, shrank away like a craven, although the earl offered to allow the dastard to come armed from head to foot against him in hose and jerkin, to encourage him the rather to accept the challenge. Bagnal was valiant enough with the pen, when inditing charges of covert treason against Tyrone; a perfect master of fence, when nothing but the pen was needed to deal an assassin thrust; but when there was a question of cold, glittering steel, his heart melted within him like wax. In fact, like the pedant King James, who now reigns, he trembled at sight of a drawn sword." (*Dialogue between two Franciscans in the city of Louvain, August 16th, 1617, according to the version of* Rev. C. P. Meehan, M. R. I. A., *in his "Rise and Fall of the Franciscan Monasteries, etc"* Dublin, 1869.)

OWEN ROE O'NEILL.

BATTLE OF BENBURB.

Owen Roe McArt O'Neill was a worthy scion of the royal Ulster house of that name, and one of the bravest and most accomplished captains, not only of the Irish race, but of his period, in Europe; so much so, that Napoleon is said to have expressed his opinion that, if his life had been spared, he would have been more than a match for the infamous, but warlike Cromwell. In A. D. 1641, the Irish, goaded into insurrection by cruelty and persecution, rose in arms, and, in the following year, Owen Roe, then serving with great distinction in the Spanish army, was invited to Ireland to take command of the northern forces. In June, 1642, he sailed homeward from Dunkirk, and in a few days, landed at Donegal. The enemy in Ulster at the time consisted of about thirteen thousand troops, mostly Scotchmen, commanded by Major-General Robert Monro, while the forces, which the patriots could place at the disposal of their new general, did not, at most, number over fifteen hundred. O'Neill's strategy, therefore, was to avoid a general engagement, and by a series of brilliant skirmishes to give confidence and steadiness to his fresh levies. In this he succeeded admirably, and at the end of four years he felt himself strong enough to cope with his adversary.

On Friday, the 5th of June, 1646, the collision of the opposing forces took place near the church of Benburb, county of Tyrone, in the angle formed by the rivers Blackwater and Oonagh. The Irish troops numbered five thousand infantry and five hundred cavalry, while Monro's, which have been variously estimated at from three thousand four hundred to eight thousand five hundred, actually consisted of some seven thousand, of whom eight hundred were mounted, with seven pieces of cannon. What Owen Roe, however, lacked in numbers, he made up in quality, if we can judge from the following names of his subordinates, who constituted the flower of the northern and western chivalry of that day.

They were Sir Phelim O'Neill and his brother Thurlough; Con, Cormac, Hugh and Brian O'Neill; and the following chieftains with their clans: Bernard MacMahon the son of Hugh, Chief of Monaghan, and Baron of Dartry; Colonel MacMahon, Colonel Patrick MacNeney, Colonel Richard O'Ferrall of Longford, Roger Maguire of Fermanagh, Colonel Philip O'Reilly of Ballynacargy Castle in the county of Cavan, and Maolmora O'Kelly (Miles the Slasher). The O'Reillys brought two hundred chosen men of their own name, and of the MacBradys, M'Cabes, MacGowans, Fitzpatricks, and Fitzsimons from Cavan. Some fighting men were also brought by MacGauran of Templeport and MacTeirnan of Croghan; some Connaught forces came with the O'Rourkes, McDermotts, O'Connors, O'Kellys, and the O'Donnells and O'Dougherties of Donegal; Manus O'Kane of Derry; Sir Constantine Magennis of Down, the O'Hanlons of Armagh, and the O'Hagans of Tyrone.*

In the spring of 1646, O'Neill marched into the county of Armagh, and was followed by Monro, who hoped by a surprise to catch him in the city of that name. At the same time he ordered his brother, Colonel George Monro, from Coleraine by the west side of Lough Neagh with three troops of horse, to join him at Glass Lough in the County of Monaghan. The Irish general hearing this, resolved to prevent the junction, and evacuating Armagh, marched on a place called Bally Kilgavan, where, having taken up a position, he dispatched some cavalry, under Colonels McMahon and MacNeney, to check George Monro's advance, and drive him back on Dungannon: a work which was handsomely accomplished.

Meanwhile Monro, with the main body of his army, marched through the city of Armagh and up the right bank of the river Blackwater; and O'Neill, according to previous intention, fell back on the Blackwater,

* Davis.

where he resolved to give battle. His position was well chosen, his right flank resting on a wet bog, and his left protected by the two rivers, while in his front the ground was covered with hillocks and clumps of wood as covers for skirmishers. Monro crossed the Blackwater at Kinaird (Caledon), and advanced down the left bank to the attack. These manœuvres occupied nearly the entire day, so that it was after four o'clock in the afternoon before the advance of the enemy came in contact with the Irish outposts. At first, the advantage seemed to be on the side of the Anglo-Scotch troops. O'Farrell's cavalry were driven in; the skirmishers, after doing considerable damage, were obliged to retreat; the Scotch musketeers for a time caused great havoc on the left, and Monro's artillery played with effect on the centre. It was at this crisis that O'Neill's generalship and continental training became conspicuous. Forming two lines of infantry into a column of attack, with the cavalry in the interstice, he gave the order for a general charge, and his men with a wild cheer rushed up the hill upon the foe, and without firing a shot (a favorite movement it seems with our countrymen), dashed in on the enemy's infantry and cavalry indiscriminately. This charge could not be withstood, and though stubbornly met, the result was not long doubtful. While the infantry was thus engaged, the Irish cavalry, deploying to the right and left, wheeled into line on Monro's flanks, charged simultaneously on the disorganized masses, and completed the victory. The havoc was immense for the numbers engaged, and shows what training existed on one side, and desperation on the other. No less than *three thousand four hundred and twenty three* of the enemy fell on the field; and Lord Montgomery, with twenty-one officers and one hundred and fifty men, were taken prisoners. Owen Roe lost in all seventy killed, including Colonels Manus O'Kane, MacNeill, and Garve O'Donnell, and two hundred wounded, including several officers. All the enemy's artillery, small arms, twenty stand of colors, ammunition, provisions and fifteen hundred draught-horses became the spoils of the victors. General rejoicing prevailed through Ireland on the receipt of the news of this splendid victory; and Owen Roe O'Neill's name was on every tongue, and his praise became, and is to this day, the theme of many a song and tale.

A FIGHTING BISHOP.

THE CONFEDERATION OF KILKENNY.

However modern notions of propriety may be shocked at the idea of a Catholic prelate exchanging the crozier for the sword, it cannot be denied that in the early Christian ages many pious and illustrious ecclesiastics took up arms to defend the Church and to crush its infidel and idolatrous enemies. Bishop McMahon, of whose career we abridge the following sketch from a recent work by the Rev. C. P. Meehan,* inherited the fiery zeal of those holy prelates, and fought for a cause as sacred as that which called Italy to arms against the Goths, or poured upon the plains and hills of Palestine the flower of European chivalry. We have preferred to give as near as possible

* *The Franciscan Monasteries and the Irish Hierarchy of the 17th century.* By the Rev. C. P. Meehan. Dublin, 1869.

Father Meehan's own words, as from his long study of the subjects treated in his valuable little book, and his intense, though judicious patriotism, he is more fitted than any man living, to describe the plans and actions of such a man as the valiant Bishop of Clogher, and to draw correct deductions therefrom.

Heber, or Emeric, son of Turlough MacMahon and Eva O'Neill, was born in Monaghan, in 1600. Heber's father had fought on the side of the northern chieftains, from the beginning of the war which the latter waged against Queen Elizabeth; and on every field, from Clontibret to the great victory of the Blackwater, he acted the part of a brave soldier, proving himself on all occasions a worthy representative of an ancient race, always renowned for valorous achievements. The child Heber was only seven years old when his kinsman, James Colla MacMahon, was obliged to join the Earls in their flight from Lough Swilly; and, in the course of a few years afterwards, his father was reduced to comparative poverty by the bill of attainder, which proscribed the fugitives and their adherents, and confiscated the best part of Ulster to the crown. Obliged to seek shelter, with the survivors of O'Neill's and O'Donnell's clansmen, in the then almost inaccessible wilds of Donegal, Turlough, with his wife Eva and their only child, fixed his residence in the vicinity of Killybegs, and there lived as best they could, hoping that he would, sooner or later, be restored to some parcel of those grand domains which had been so cruelly and unjustly wrested from him and his. News, however, reached Ireland towards the close of 1608, that James MacMahon and his companion in misfortune, Lord Maguire, had died immediately after their arrival at Genoa; and the Executive, acting on this welcome intelligence, confirmed the grant of Turlough's patrimony to the new occupier, and thus annulled all the claims of the rightful owner. At that period, Turlough was too old to take service in the Spanish armies; and as he was suffering from wounds received on the disastrous day of Kinsale, he resolved to remain at home, and devote the remainder of his days to the initiating young Heber, his sole hope, in the rudiments of the military profession till the lad would be fit to sail for Flanders, and there enlist into the Irish regiment, which was then commanded by the eldest son of the banished Earl of Tyrone. Heber, indeed, did inherit the chivalrous instincts of his father; but his mother, it would appear, had no ambition to see him trailing halberd or lance; and she consequently resolved that his hopes and aspirations should take an opposite direction, and yearn for the still higher honor of serving in the weakened ranks of the Church, then truly *militant*, in Ireland. Heber seconded his mother's wishes, and laid down sword and target for book and pen; and that nothing might be wanting to forward his education, she called into her humble homestead a Franciscan friar of Donegal, who, in return for the bread and shelter afforded him, taught the boy Latin, Greek, and Spanish, and made him thoroughly familiar with the history of his unfortunate country. Towards the close of 1617, Heber set out for Douay, and entered the Irish college, which Cussack, a priest of Meath, had endowed in that old Flemish town. Having completed his philosophical course there, he removed to Louvain, in order to avail himself of the lectures of the learned Franciscan, MacCaghwell, who was then esteemed one of the most profound theologians of his time. At length, having gone through the prescribed cycle of studies, and attained his twenty-fifth year, Heber was ordained priest in the chapel of the Irish Franciscan convent at Louvain; John Colgan, Donatus Mooney, Father O'Cleary, and other celebrities assisting on the occasion.

At the time of his ordination, Louvain, and, indeed, every other garrison town in Flanders, swarmed with Irish troops, commanded by Owen Roe O'Neill, Preston, of the house of Gormanston, O'Cahan, and others, who were destined to take part in the eventful vicissitudes of their native land at a future period. Had MacMahon wished to remain among his exiled countrymen, he could easily have found advancement at the hands of the archdukes, Albert and Isabella, then the steadiest friends of the Irish Catholics; but, knowing that his services were required in the land of his birth, he hastened home, and devoted himself with heroic zeal to the duties of his calling. On his arrival in his native diocese, he found the Catholics deprived not only of their lands, but of their churches, and obliged to assist at the divine sacrifice wherever it could be celebrated, without attracting the notice of the "Undertakers," in the recesses of the mountains, and oftener still on the hillsides which commanded a view of the surrounding districts, and enabled them to take precaution against being surprised or interrupted. The people respected MacMahon not only as a priest, but as one of the representatives of the ancient nobility of Ulster who had suffered so much for religion and country; and we may easily imagine with what weight his words fell on their hearts, when he exhorted them to persevere in the same profession, and beseech God to take compassion on their endurance. Cautiously avoiding all overt acts that could provoke the intolerance of Lord Falkland, and the deputies who succeeded him, he toiled as a simple priest twenty years in the diocese of Clogher; and so efficiently,. that O'Reilly, vicar-apostolic of Kilmore, and subsequently archbishop of Armagh, wrote to Rome that he deserved the highest honors to which the Holy See could advance him The primate, doubtless, regarded him as eminently qualified to preside over the ancient see of Clogher; in a word, as one whose election to that dignity would be hailed with delight by the people, who, in the midst of their reverses, still maintained traditional reverence for the son of the Orgiellian chieftains.

At the commencement of the agitation which heralded the insurrection of 1641, MacMahon signified to Lord Ormond that the Catholics of the north, unable to bear the oppressions of the Scotch and English undertakers, would assuredly rise in arms, unless the Executive took means to protect their lives against the repeated acts of aggression to which they were hourly exposed; but this timely warning was utterly thrown away on Parsons and Borlase, whose aim was to goad the "papists" to rebellion, in order that they might share between them the remnant of property that was still in the hands of the latter. At length, however, endurance reached its extremest limit; the northern Catholics appealed to arms; and among those who were involved in the abortive attempt to seize Dublin Castle and the persons of the Lords Justices, was Hugh MacMahon, the near kinsman of the subject of this memoir.

At the outbreak of the revolution, Father Heber exerted all his power and influence to restrain the licentiousness of the multitudes who flocked to the standard of Sir Phelim O'Neill and the other northern leaders; and such were his exertions in behalf of the Protestants, that many of them owed their lives and preservation of their property to his charitable interference. As soon, however, as the "rising" assumed the character of a general movement, he co-operated with Archbishop O'Reilly and the other prelates who assembled at Kells, and finally at Kilkenny, to direct the people in laying the foundations of the confederacy. On all these occasions, the prelates and lay lords gave attentive ear to his suggestions, and regarded him as one whose wisdom was only equalled by his well-known courage. At length, when the confederacy was fully organized, and the prelates had resolved to fill those sees that were vacant, a memorial was forwarded to Rome, praying his Holiness, Urban VIII, to promote MacMahon to the bishopric of Clogher, as no other could be found more deserving of such advancement, either by ancient descent or grand services rendered to the new government. The Holy See granted the prayer of the petitioners, and MacMahon was consecrated at Drogheda, early in 1643, after having held the see of Down and Connor as *bishop-elect* for two years previously.

The motives that determined this selection were twofold—spiritual and temporal—for the Holy See not only appreciated the services which MacMahon had rendered to religion, but set due value on his acknowledged influence with the people of his province, who recognized him as the representative of their ancient chieftains, and were nowise loath to follow him to the field, whenever he might find it imperative to lay aside crook and mitre for sword and helmet. In fact, he was the fittest man for the dignity to which he was elevated, for it is likely that no other could have been found at the time possessing so many attributes of a militant prelate. His first essay in that capacity was made a year before he received the bull appointing him to the see of Clogher, when he marched at the head of a strong detachment of troops, to congratulate his early friend, Owen O'Neill, on his arrival in Ireland, and tender to that brave general the aid of his sword whenever he might need it. Strange as such a proposition may appear to us, it could not shock or surprise O'Neill, who, doubtless, was aware that many Spanish and Italian prelates, and Pope Julius II especially, had dared death in the field; and he therefore accepted the chivalrous offer with a soldier's thankfulness.

But what O'Neill desired most at that juncture was the removal of his kinsman, Sir Phelim, from the command of the Ulster forces, and to have at his disposal large levies of stalwart youths, who, when disciplined after the Spanish fashion, were to be officered by those gallant and experienced men who had seen service with him in many a campaign and shared his laurels at Arras. It is almost unnecessary to say, that Father Heber voted Owen Roe general-in-chief of the northern confederates, and spared no effort to procure recruits for that chieftain's standard, till he had the satisfaction of seeing him at the head of a large and highly disciplined army. Such truly valuable services were fully recognized at Rome, where Father Wadding, and others not less influential, commended them to the notice of the Holy See; and we have glanced at them here in order to explain why it was that Rinuccini was instructed to make a confidant of Heber, bishop of Clogher. The first meeting of these two personages took place in the castle of Kilkenny, immediately after the nuncio's arrival in that city, and then commenced that friendship and continuity of intercourse, which lasted through so many years of triumph and reverses. Indeed, one of the nuncio's earliest despatches shows that MacMahon realized his ideal of a true and energetic bishop; for when enumerating the many difficulties he had to encounter from the opposition of the older prelates, who made small account of "the splendor of religion, through fear of not being able to maintain it," he reports to the Holy See that the *recently* consecrated bishop of Clogher was most anxious for the restoration of the splendor and publicity of ecclesiastical ceremonies; and that that personage, although guided by political precedents, afforded a marked contrast to the old bishops, who, having passed through the days of persecution, were constantly haunted by a dread that such times might come again. They lacked resolution and boldness, but in the person of MacMahon he found all that he could desire,—a will conformable to his own, and a spirit of daring, that was always prepared to encounter the most formidable emergencies.

MacMahon, although occupying the place of a spiritual peer in the supreme council, was not advanced to the temporalities of his bishopric till after the battle of Benburb, when that victory gave the confederates a shortlived triumph in Ulster; but even then he resided less frequently in his diocese than in the immediate vicinity of the nuncio and the camp of Owen O'Neill, who was entirely directed and influenced by his counsels. As might be expected, MacMahon subscribed the rejection of the peace of 1646, and took an active part in the congregation of the clergy at Waterford, where the bishops assumed the government, under the presidency of the nuncio, and committed the sad blunder of calling O'Neill's army from the pursuit of the Scotch puritans to support the new régime. Thenceforth he became, if possible, still more devoted to the nuncio, approved all his projects, and maintained that his policy and Owen O'Neill's sword were the sole means for rescuing Ireland from present and future oppression.

Acting on this conviction, he caused O'Neill to signify to the nuncio that the preponderating military power which the victory of Benburb had secured for him, was entirely at his service, and that the Ulster forces were ready to march on Dublin whenever he might think fit to sanction that enterprise. The reduction of the capital, we need hardly say, was one of Rinuccini's most cherished projects, and as MacMahon was well aware of this, he insisted that no time should be lost in making the attempt. The nuncio hesitated, not, indeed, through apprehension of failure, but rather from fear of giving umbrage to Queen Henrietta Maria, then at Paris; and it was not till after several weeks of inaction he resolved to summon the metropolis to surrender.

In the beginning of autumn, 1646, O'Neill advanced with his Ulster men through the north of Leinster, and being joined by the forces under Preston, they pitched their camps at Leixlip and Newcastle, while the nuncio and MacMahon took up their quarters in the immediate vicinity, to hasten the operations of the two generals. Acting on the advice of Castlehaven, Ormond wasted the country all around before he retired into Dublin; and as the winter had set in with unusual severity, the confederates were but ill supplied with provisions. Worst of all, the old jealousies between Preston and O'Neill had broken out afresh; and to add to this complication of difficulties, Lord Clanricarde, a Catholic and hitherto neutral, appeared on the scene to tamper with Preston, whose hatred of O'Neill was only equalled by his want of firmness. In the midst of these dissensions, the nuncio felt himself bewildered, and apprehending that he must lose all chance of taking Dublin if he failed to unite the two generals, he went, accompanied by the bishop of Clogher, to Preston's quarters, to effect a mutual understanding. The Leinster general behaved on this occasion with marked reserve, and though he had been urged to arrest the bishop of Clogher, he refused to do so. The conference, however, did not bring about the desired reconciliation; and much as the nuncio plumed himself on his courage in traversing the level country north of the city, "where a few straggling horsemen might have picked him up and carried him to Lord Ormond," all his efforts went for nothing; so much so that, on a rumor of a parliamentary squadron having dropped anchor in the bay, O'Neill and Preston struck their tents and retired hastily in the direction of Kilkenny.

At length, however, when news reached him that Preston had been defeated at Trim by Jones, to whom Lord Ormond surrendered Dublin for a sum of thirteen thousand pounds, he wrote to Owen O'Neill to march with his army, and save Kilkenny from the parliamentary forces. The Ulster general gladly obeyed the summons, marched rapidly on Trim, occupied the ground where Preston had been so shamefully routed, and kept Jones's troops in check for fully four months. The bold manœuvre was, indeed, the salvation of the confederates; for O'Neill's sudden appearance on the scene of the late disaster caused Jones to retire within the walls of Dublin, and abandon his design of reducing Kilkenny. MacMahon joined the Ulster general at Trim, and remained constantly in his camp till summoned by the nuncio to Kilkenny, to take part in the momentous debates which at that period distracted the confederate councils.

At the close of 1647, the Ormondist faction resolved, if possible, to get rid of the nuncio and his adherents; and, in order to accomplish this, they gave out that the recent losses and widespread poverty from which the whole country was suffering could not be remedied, except by appealing to the Pope and other potentates for assistance in money and munitions. It was also suggested that the terms proposed by Ormond, in 1646, should be reconsidered and accepted, provided the guarantees for religion were amplified; and finally, that deputations should be sent to the various Catholic courts, to represent the miserable condition of the confederates, and obtain whatever aids they might be disposed to advance. This, indeed, was an adroit *ruse* to get shut of Rinuccini's partisans, and, according to the programme, it was voted and carried in the assembly, that MacMahon should proceed, with Lord Muskerry and Doctor Brown, to the court of Queen Henrietta Maria at Paris. The bishop, however, saw through the scheme, and resolved to defeat it. He, therefore, besought the council to substitute one in his place; "For," said he, "I am ignorant of the French and English languages, and the queen has conceived strong prejudices to me, as it has been told her that I took an active part in promoting this war, and rejecting the peace of 1646. Moreover, I have reason to think that I would be hazarding my life were I to undertake this mission; for Digby, the queen's secretary, and her special favorite, St. Germain, are my sworn enemies. Find some one else for this business; for nothing shall induce me to embark in it." This declaration surprised and confounded the Ormondists; and so indignant were Muskerry, Taaff, Preston, and others, that they waited on the mayor of Kilkenny, and charged him to have the bishop of Clogher placed under arrest for contumacy and breach of privilege. The mayor, however, instead of doing as they commanded, made the bishop an offer of his protection, alleging as his reason for doing so, that he did not feel himself bound to obey the order of the assembly in this instance. On hearing this, Preston left the city to assemble his troops that were encamped in the neighborhood; detachments of the garrison were turned out to patrol the streets, and the gates were closed to keep the bishop or any of his friends from communicating with O'Neill, whose tents were visible from the ramparts of the city. Next day, however, MacMahon took his place in the assembly; but such was the excitement provoked by his appearance, that he was forced to retire while the Ormondists were gravely discussing the legality of committing him to prison. That, indeed, was a serious question; and those who were for incarcerating him cited countless precedents, furnished by history and the statute book; but, as the bishops then present demurred to such special pleading, the Ormondists insisted that a written order should be sent to MacMahon, forbidding him to leave the city The bishops, however, would not sanction this; and so strenuous was their opposition, that the assembly caused their written order to be cancelled, and commissioned their speaker to wait on MacMahon, and request him not to go beyond the walls. Irritated by this untoward proceeding, the nuncio insisted that the Ormondists had "violated ecclesiastical immunity," and were, consequently, bound to make reparation for their error, if they were not prepared to encounter the resentment of Owen O'Neill, who, in his camp at Maryborough, told the agent of the French court that he would never set foot in Kilkenny till ample apology had been made to the offended prelate, who was his especial friend and adviser. Alarmed at this, the assembly made the required atonement, and appointed the Marquis of Antrim to be one of the deputation in lieu of the bishop of Clogher, whose presence in Ireland was indispensably necessary at that moment, when Rinuccini was about to resort to those extreme measures, for the enforcement of which he required the aid of the carnal weapon.

It is almost superfluous to say that the Bishop of Clogher figured prominently in the council of prelates who rejected Inchiquin's truce, and from fourteen of whom Rinuccini procured a conditional power, to excommunicate all favorers of that overture, in conjunction with four specified bishops, or in case of their non-attendance, with four to be named by himself. Indeed, in this instance, MacMahon did nothing more than what might have been expected from one whose antecedents proved that he was devotedly attached to the nuncio throughout, and the more so as the latter had always shown a decided preference for Owen O'Neill and the Catholics of Ulster. Actuated by such sentiments, he aided the nuncio in effecting his escape from Kilkenny, and accompanied him to O'Neill's camp at Maryborough, where he tarried some time meditating what was best to be done at such a moment, and how he might be able to make his final exit from Ireland. Sad and perilous, indeed, was Rinuccini's sojourn with Owen Roe, for the forces which were then at his disposal could not cope with the united armies of Preston and Inchiquin, had they marched on Maryborough; but far more poignant than the apprehension he entertained of being surprised and utterly routed by his sworn enemies, was the intimation which Rinuccini gave him of his approaching departure from the kingdom. O'Neill implored him to abandon his intention, and MacMahon urged that the great body of the clergy, notwithstanding the political defection of eight bishops, and three-fourths of the entire population, still adhered to his cause. But all in vain; for Rinuccini clearly saw that no permanent benefit could come of his presence in Ireland, and that he was utterly powerless to bring about a union of the conflicting parties who were more intent on sacrificing each other than acting in concert for the common good. Full of this conviction, he took leave of O'Neill, and proceeded to Athlone, where, on the refusal of the four authorized bishops to sanction his last and most daring measure, he summoned four others in their stead, and with their consent pronounced sentence of excommunication against the abettors of Inchiquin's truce, and laid all parts of the kingdom, where it would be accepted, under interdict. The bishop of Clogher subscribed the sentence, and had the gratification of learning soon afterwards that two thousand of Preston's soldiers, terrified by the Church's thunders, had deserted that general, and ranged themselves under O'Neill's standard. Elated by this momentary success, and exasperated by the Ormondists, who pronounced him guilty of high treason, O'Neill broke up his camp at Maryborough, and proceeded northwards, in order to reënforce his little army. On this expedition he was accompanied by the bishop of Clogher, and such was the enthusiasm of the Ulstermen for both chieftain and prelate, that O'Neill soon found himself at the head of ten thousand infantry and fifteen hundred horse, indifferently armed it is true, but ready and willing to follow wherever their general might be disposed to lead them. With this contingent O'Neill and the bishop returned to Leinster, routed Preston, and then advanced by forced marches into the county Tipperary, where four thousand brave peasants enrolled themselves under the confederate banners, and solemnly pledged themselves to stand by the cause of the "old Irish" and the Church. Nenagh, Banagher, and other strong places on the Shannon were speedily in the power of O'Neill's troops, and in this brief but brilliant campaign, the nuncio tells us that the Ulster chieftain defeated seven generals who were opposed to him, and thus, for the fifth time, saved religion and Ireland from the enemies of both. Having accomplished all this, O'Neill and the bishop returned to the north, to protect the people of that province from the inroads of the Parliamentarians.

Meanwhile, Lord Ormond had resumed the government, and signified to the nuncio that he must quit the kingdom without further delay. The intimation was soon followed by that personage's departure for the shores of France, and O'Neill and his faithful adherent, the bishop of Clogher, were left to take whatever course they deemed best for the good of the country and their own preservation. Finding himself thus abandoned by his former friends, and driven to desperation by want of provisions and military supplies, O'Neill was constrained to accept the overtures of Sir Charles Coote, who proposed to furnish him with a considerable quantity of powder and ball, on condition that he would march to the relief of Derry, then besieged by the Scotch, under Lord Montgomery. O'Neill accepted the offer, marched against the Scotch, who fled across the Bann at his approach, and was splendidly entertained at Derry by Coote, who professed himself under lasting obligations to his deliverer. This unnatural alliance, which nothing but extreme necessity could justify, was not destined to last, for the English Parliament rebuked Coote for treating with O'Neill; and the latter, disgusted with the hostility he experienced from those whom had he so generously relieved, resolved to break with them, and make a tender of his services to Lord Ormond. During his short sojourn at Derry, O'Neill was seized with a mortal malady, occasioned, it was said, however unwarrantably, by poison, with which Coote caused his wine to be drugged, or, as others would have it, by a pair of poisoned russet boots, sent him by one Plunket of Louth, and in this condition he had to be carried in a horse-litter to Cloughouter, the residence of his brother-in-law, Colonel Philip O'Reilly. O'Neill's sufferings were painful, and, despite the science of the many physicians who strove to save him, he sank gradually, "his hair and nails falling off," and expired on the sixth of November, 1649. The bishop of Clogher never left the gallant patient's bedside during his protracted illness, but remained constantly there preparing him for the "doubtful transit," and "receiving his last instructions for the maintenance of the Ulster army." Two days after the melancholy event, O'Reilly, the primate, Magennis, bishop of Down, and Heber, of Clogher, accompanied by all the kinsmen and officers of the deceased, followed his mortal remains to the Franciscan monastery of Cavan, and there committed them to a grave which, from that time to the present, has not had a single stone to distinguish it, and, doubtless, must remain so till the Irish people shall have learnt to worship the memory of their true heroes.

Being thus deprived of their general, the officers of the Ulster army resolved that no time should be lost in electing some one to fill his place, and they accordingly assembled for that purpose at Belturbet, early in March, 1650. The meeting was held in the house of MacSweeny, bishop of Kilmore, who was named to preside on the momentous occasion. Among those present were the marquis of Antrim, Sir Phelim O'Neill, Henry O'Neill, Con MacCormack O'Neill, Lieutenant-General O'Farrell, Philip MacHugh O'Reilly, Heber, bishop of Clogher, the bishop of Down, and many other ecclesiastics. The O'Neills contended that the generalship belonged of right to them, and that it was hereditary in their family. O'Farrel, on the other hand, maintained that he, as lieutenant-general to Owen Roe, was entitled to the command; and the Marquis of Antrim pressed his own claims, which he grounded on the intimacy that had so long subsisted between himself and Owen Roe, to whom he had rendered many signal services. The debate was protracted and stormy; and the assembly, considering the danger that was likely to ensue by electing any of the aforesaid, even Henry, son of the deceased general, and the most deserving of all, resolved to put an end to future intrigue, by nominating Heber, bishop of Clogher, to the vacancy. As matter of course, this selection could not please all parties, for some asserted that MacMahon was not equal to the requirements of the situation, and others, not having the fear of the consequences before their eyes, and affecting to be scandalized, did not shrink from asserting that the combination of crook and sword was a thing which no true Catholic could stomach. Withal, as there was no remedy for this seeming incongruity, they resolved to follow wheresoever the bishop would lead them, for they knew that he was the depositary of Owen O'Neill's confidence, and fully cognizant of the treaty which the latter had concluded with Lord Ormond just one month before his decease.

Having now assumed the command, the bishop lost no time in mustering his troops, and being joined by detachments of Ulstermen, drafted from the garrison of Waterford, and several regiments which had seen service in Leinster and Connaught, under O'Cahan and other distinguished officers, he marched into the county Monaghan at the head of an army amounting to about 5,000 foot and 600 horse. The influence of MacMahon's name and lineage in his native province caused multitudes of young recruits to rally round his standard, and, in the course of a few months, he had the satisfaction of seeing his available force largely increased, and well-disciplined by O'Farrell, whose commission of lieutenant-general had been confirmed by the Belturbet council. Leaving that officer in temporary command, the bishop proceeded to Loughreagh, in order to take counsel with Lords Ormond and Clanricarde, and procure for them such aids as were required for carrying on the war against Sir Charles Coote, Venables, and other leaders, who, notwithstanding the recent murder of king Charles I and the proclaiming of his successor, still stood out in open rebellion to the king. Ormond received the bishop cordially, condoled with him on the death of O'Neill, in whose honor, he said, he always placed implicit trust; and, after congratulating him as successor to the deceased general, confirmed the appointment with a commission of the following tenor:—

"To our trusty and well-beloved bishop, *Ever MacMahon.*

"Ormond.

"Whereas, upon the treaty with general Owen O'Neill, deceased, it was, amongst other particulars, concluded and agreed upon, that, in case of death or removal of him, such other general or commander-in-chief should be authorized by commission from us to command his Majesty's forces of the province of Ulster, natives of the kingdom, as should be by general consent of the gentry of that province elected and made choice of for the same. And whereas, in a general meeting lately held by the gentry for that purpose, it was agreed upon, and represented unto us, that you should exercise that command over the said forces, we, therefore, upon the consideration thereof, and of the care, judgment, valor, and experience in martial affairs, as also of the readiness and good affections of you to do his majesty service, have nominated and appointed, and we do hereby nominate and appoint you, the said bishop, *Ever MacMahon*, to be general of all his Majesty's said forces of horse and foot, of the province of Ulster, natives of the kingdom. Given, &c., &c."

Having concerted with Ormond and Clanricarde the plan of the approaching campaign, and obtained from them assurance of plentiful supplies of field artillery, victuals, and ammunition, MacMahon returned to Monaghan, and placing himself at the head of his army, marched on Charlemont, where he and his chief officers published a manifesto, in which they invited the Scots to forget the animosities that had hitherto existed between them and the Irish, and to sink all distinction of nation and *religion* for the sake of the royal interest and service. Many of the Scots were converted to royalism by this appeal, but the great majority of Coote's forces revolted at the idea of serving under the standard of a "popish bishop," no matter what side of the quarrel he chose to take, and therefore resolved to share the fortunes of their old leaders.

Seeing there was no hope of detaching the Scots from Coote and Venables, the bishop resolved to attack them in detail, and, if possible, prevent the juncture of their respective forces, as neither of them would have been able to fight him singlehanded. With this object, he marched northwards along Bann, stormed Dungiven, Ballycastle, and other places of no great importance, and finally crossed the Foyle, near Lifford, in order to maintain a communication, through Ballyshannon, with

Connaught, whence he expected the supplies promised by Ormond and Clanricarde. This, however, proved to be a disastrous manœuvre, for it enabled Venables to send Coote, who was then encamped at Skirfolas, in the neighborhood of Letterkenny, a reinforcement of one thousand veteran soldiers, who had seen service under Monro, from the commencement of the Irish war. On the twenty-first of June, 1650, the two armies were within an hour's march of each other; and as both were pretty equally matched, the bishop resolved to risk a battle, contrary to the advice of his most experienced officers, who insisted that he should hold a council of war, and abide by the decision of the majority. To this he submitted reluctantly, and while he and his chiefs were engaged in discussing the momentous question, a woman of uncommon stature, gaunt and dressed in white, forced her way into their midst, and quoted an old prophecy which foretold that the Irish were doomed to be overthrown on the banks of the Swilly. MacMahon, however, paid little heed to the crazed virago, and, perhaps, less to the unanswerable arguments of Henry Roe O'Neill, who urged that instead of engaging the enemy on broken ground where the Irish troops could not act with precision, it would be more prudent to wait till the former should be obliged, through want of provisions, to shift their quarters, when it would be easy to fall on them, and cut them up in detail. It was also urged, that the force at the bishop's disposal had been weakened by the absence of a large body which he detached to seize Castle Doe; but all arguments were thrown away upon him, for he was obstinate as he was rashly brave. The attack of the Irish was impetuous, but, as Henry O'Neill had foretold, the rugged and stony nature of the ground would not suffer them to act in compact masses, and notwithstanding all their chivalry, they were taken in flank and rear by Coote's forces, who, in the course of a few hours, routed them with slaughter. Eighteen captains of the O'Farrells were slain on the fatal field, and fifteen hundred of the common soldiers perished before the fire of Coote's musketeers. Henry O'Neill and many others of his name and kindred were captured, and brought to Derry, where Coote had them summarily executed, after quarter given, and notwithstanding the heavy ransom which was offered for their lives.

As for Bishop McMahon, he contrived to make his escape from the bloody field of Letterkenny, in company with Lieutenant-General O'Farrell, and some squadrons of horse, riding day and night, without meat or drink, for twenty-four hours, till he and his jaded followers reached the neighborhood of Enniskillen, where they were set upon by a detachment of the garrison. The bishop's escort offered what resistance they could, but were soon obliged to yield to superior force, and surrender at discretion. He himself was severely wounded in this last action, and so was O'Farrell; but less fortunate than the latter, who made his escape, MacMahon was carried prisoner to Enniskillen, and there committed to the common jail, to wait Coote's final sentence.

The close of MacMahon's career was such as might have been expected from one, a goodly portion of whose life had been divided between the church and the camp; and much as the Cromwellian troopers admired his undaunted resolution, they never were so deeply impressed by it as on that July evening when they escorted him to the ancient castle of Enniskillen,—the place appointed for his execution. Marching some paces in advance of the musketeers, his bearing was calm, dignified, and martial, so much so, that a casual wayfarer might have mistaken him for the officer in command, were it not for the presence of an ecclesiastic, with whom he conversed in tones inaudible to every one else, and a small gold crucifix that he kept constantly moving between his lips and eyes. On reaching the scaffold he knelt and prayed in silence for a while, and then, turning to the troops who kept the ground, told them that he thanked God for having given him that opportunity of laying down his life in the cause of religion, king, and country. MacMahon's soul had scarcely gone to its account, when the executioner, in compliance with the barbarous usage of the times, flung the corse to the ground, hacked off the head, and spiked it on the tower of the castle, where it remained till birds of prey, rain, storm, and time destroyed every vestige of the ghastly trophy. The mutilated trunk, however, had a sympathizing Catholic to convey it to Devenish Island, where it waits the resurrection, under the shadow of St. Laserian's oratory.

PATRICK SARSFIELD.

DEFENCE OF LIMERICK.

PATRICK SARSFIELD, Earl of Lucan, whose name is perhaps more familiar in the memory of his countrymen than that of any other national soldier since the days of the "mighty Brian," was chiefly remarkable for his bravery, dash, and rapidity of conception during the Williamite wars; for his career on the continent was short, though distinguished. In mental capacity and temperament he bore a close resemblance to our own Major-General "Phil" Sheridan, though in physical proportions he was much superior to the hero of Winchester, for he was of lofty stature and possessed rare muscular power; qualities, which in his day, when hand-to-hand encounters were so frequent, were of much greater value to a commanding general than they are now.

Sarsfield learned the rudiments of his military education in France, and subsequently held a commission in the English Guards under James II, when that monarch, by the advice of Tyrconnel, recruited his army in England from the sister kingdom, and, despite the penal laws, appointed a great many Catholic officers to command in it. When William of Orange landed in England, Sarsfield returned to Ireland; and when James arrived there from France to make a last effort for the throne, he received the appointment of Brigadier-General, his command consisting of mixed infantry and calvary, but principally of the latter. At the head of those troops during the siege of Derry and the entire campaign of 1689, he did most efficient service, scouring the northern and western counties, cutting off marauding parties and other detachments of the enemy, and capturing provisions and military stores. His activity was so great as to give an air of ubiquity to his person, and he was known to have appeared with his rough-riders in places fifty or sixty miles apart in the space of twenty-four hours: a feat which, considering the badness of the roads and the condition of the country at that time, necessarily created a good deal of astonishment among friends and enemies.

At the battle of the Boyne he was equally distinguished for his tact and impetuous charges. With Berwick and Hamilton, he commanded King James's horse on that disastrous day, and was ever found in the thick of the fight; right, left, or centre, wherever danger threatened, or his comrades seemed about to be overpowered, his presence was sure to be the signal of success. Like the illustrious Henry of Navarre, his plume was the standard round which the soldiers fought—at least those of Irish birth. It was, however, in the defence of the city of Limerick, that Lord Lucan displayed his great abilities and unshaken fortitude to the greatest advantage. After the defeat of the Boyne, the surrender of Dublin, and the flight of the timid king to France, the Irish army and its French allies retreated on the Shannon, the best line of defence in the country, and one that should have been adopted in the first instance. Athlone and Limerick, both on that river, the first commanding the road into Connaught, and the other at the head of tide water, and in uninterrupted communication with the continent, were the two principal positions to be defended; and though both were indifferently fortified, it became of the utmost consequence that they should be held, particularly the latter city. A council of war was convened, at which Lausan, the commander-in-chief, and most of the French officers were of opinion that Limerick was untenable, having at the time, according to the Duke of Berwick, " no other fortifications than a wall without ramparts and a few miserable towers without ditches." Sarsfield, Berwick, and other Irish officers of distinction differed with them; and, believing that the fall of Limerick would be fatal to their cause, declared their determination to defend it to the last extremity with their own troops, should their foreign allies abandon them. They were taken at their word, and Lausan accordingly marched off his men to the west side of the Shannon and thence to Galway, taking with him a large quantity of ammunition, supplies, &c.; and thus, weakened in men and munitions, the Irish troops were left to defend the city as best they might. They went to work, however, with great spirit; and every thing that could be done to strengthen their defences, was essayed previous to the appearance of William before its walls on the eighth day of August. Meanwhile a part of the Anglo-Dutch troops under Major-General Douglass had been sent against Athlone; but meeting with a sterner resistance from the garrison there than they were led to expect, and fearing an attack in the rear from the troops in Limerick, he raised the siege and joined William. The latter's army, when he commenced the siege, is estimated, even by English authorities, at over thirty-eight thousand, with several pieces of artillery and a plentiful supply of requisite ammunition. After taking a critical survey of the Irish position, William and his general officers resolved to commence a regular investment of the town, by throwing up works around it and establishing two batteries of five and four guns each, to dominate the frail defences of their adversaries. Unfortunately for the Irish, they were now commanded by Tyrconnel, a nobleman more accustomed to courts than camp life, and who, from ignorance or natural timidity, it is alleged, greatly embarrassed the movements of his more skilled and enterprising subordinates, Berwick and Sarsfield, to whom was left the defence of Limerick, while the commander-in-chief idled away his time with the French in Galway.

William, after a few days' bombardment, found his guns too light to make any impression on the works, and he consequently ordered from Dublin a battering train of eight heavy guns, five mortars, one hundred and fifty-three wagon loads of ammunition, eighteen tin pontoons, four hundred draught-horses, and twelve wagons filled with biscuit. This important supply train was convoyed by a mere handful of troops, probably not more than two hundred men; for so *pacified* had the intervening country become by the march of Anglo-Dutch through it, that a stronger guard was not considered necessary. All this became known to the besieged through two French deserters from the enemy; and Sarsfield, with his usual promptness, conceived the idea of intercepting and destroying the expected succors. Under the cover of the darkness of midnight, he crossed Thomond bridge at the head of six hundred of his horsemen, and, carefully avoiding the sentinels and videttes of the enemy, he gained the open country and awaited in concealment the approach of the enemy at Ballyneety in the county of Tipperary, a few miles from Limerick. William on his side had, soon after their departure, obtained information of this daring movement of the Irish, and ordered a strong body of cavalry under Sir John Lanier to prevent it. They were too late. As soon as night fell on the escort quietly encamped after a long march,

Sarsfield rode down on them with his usual impetuosity, and those of it that were not killed or wounded fled right and left. All the guns, stores, and horses fell into the hands of the victors. They loaded the cannon and mortars to the muzzle and buried them in the ground breach upwards, then placed the ammunition upon them, next the gun carriages, biscuit wagons, and pontoons, and setting fire to the whole, caused such an explosion that the sky is said to have been illuminated for several miles around, and the concussion was sensibly felt in the beleaguered city, signalling to those in the secret the success of the expedition. The horses were of course preserved, as well as a hundred others belonging to the regiment of Villiers, which were found ready saddled and were all brought into the city by Sarsfield, who, having made a detour to avoid the cavalry which had been sent to cut off his return, crossed the river at Banagher and entered the town in triumph, without having lost a man.

This, the most brilliant and, for the numbers employed, the most decisive exploit of the war, justly increased Lucan's popularity and fame, and gave renewed courage to the besieged, while the loss of such valuable munitions paralyzed for a time the efforts of William's army. At the end of a week, however, he contrived to supply his loss, by procuring another train of siege guns from Waterford, which, having been placed in the most advantageous position, were trained on the devoted city, and night and day kept thundering away at its crumbling earthworks and ruined towers. Nor were the Irish idle; for, though inferior in the number and calibre of their guns, and their ammunition reduced to fifty kegs of powder, they kept up as constant a fire on the enemy's lines as circumstances would permit.

At length the day arrived, the 27th of August, 1690, a day ever memorable in the history of Limerick and in the annals of Irish heroism, upon which William had fixed to take the place by storm. The defences had become but a confused mass of rubbish under the incessant cannonading of the previous days, and he resolved to drive out their stubborn defenders by sheer force. The Irish, on their side, anticipating the attack, prepared for it as well as it was possible. At either side of the breach were two columns of infantry, with a reserve stationed in the public square, while the Black Battery, the principal point of defence, was well manned and its guns double-shotted, to meet any emergency. Five hundred of the Irish Guards held St. John's gate, and musketeers thinly lined the trenches. The sun rises bright and fair over that city, so soon to be the scene of dreadful turmoil and carnage. William's cannon, at a given signal, open along the whole line of his works, and belch forth destruction and death. Under its cover a solid column of ten thousand veterans of many nations—English, Dutch, Danes, Brandenburgers and Enniskilleners (the latter the forefathers of our modern Orangemen)—advance on the Irish works with a pluck and steadiness that argue mischief for their heroic defenders. First come the British Grenadiers, supported by the Dutch Guards, the two best regiments in the army. They are allowed to approach in silence, and even to pass over the *debris* of the stockades, when the guns of the Black Battery open on them at short range. The fire is terribly destructive, their ranks are decimated, and they pause in dismay and consternation. This is the signal for an oblique fire on either flank from the infantry posted at the breach, in the ditches, and even in the windows of the adjoining houses. Still, like brave men, the grenadiers and guards rally and renew the attack, with the same result. The British are almost annihilated, and the Dutch have suffered heavily. But wave after wave succeeds, and the Irish, exhausted, weakened, and overpowered, give way, the trenches are captured, a portion of the streets is occupied by the enemy, and the last stronghold of the patriots, the Black Battery, has been captured by the Brandenburgers after a bloody struggle. The day seemed to be lost irretrievably. So at least thought William, and so, perhaps, thought also the defenders, but Berwick and Sarsfield. The latter, having foreseen the probability of such a result, had prepared for the emergency. The Battery had been mined. The moment had now come when it should be sprung. Just as the colonel of the Brandenburgers is waving his sword in triumph, and his men are cheering for the supposed victory, a low rumbling noise like that of an earthquake is heard beneath their feet, and ere one of that devoted regiment had time to say, "Lord have mercy on me," they are hurled lifeless and shattered into the air, and their dismembered limbs are falling in showers upon their late companions-in-arms.

The pause which ensued was more dreadful than the tumult that preceded it, but it was Sarsfield's opportunity. Rallying his broken columns, and placing himself conspicuously at their head, he renewed the defence; and driving the assailants from street to street, he forced them over the works into the river, and, such as remained of them, back to their camp, defeated and disorganized. Not only did the men of the town not in arms, but the women and even the children, it is said, shared in the glory of this rescue of the Saragossa of Ireland; and many young and delicately nurtured ladies were found after the combat amongst the slain by the side of their fathers, husbands, brothers, and sweethearts. Story, a very partial English historian, says of this attack and repulse:—" The Irish then ventured upon the breach again; and from the walls and every place so pestered us upon the counterscarp, that after nigh three hours resisting bullets, stones (broken bottles from the very women, who boldly stood in the breach and were nearer to our men than their own), and whatever ways could be thought on to destroy us, our ammunition being spent, it was judged safest to return to our trenches."* Those Limerick women,

* Imp. Hist., p. 129.

the descendants of whom are still so famed for their grace and delicacy, were the mothers and sisters of many of the gallant soldiers of the Brigade. To them might well be applied Byron's eulogy on the Spanish heroine:—

> "Her lover sinks—she sheds no ill-timed tear;
>   Her chief is slain—she fills his fatal post;
>   Her fellows flee—she checks their base career;
>   The foe retires—she heads the rallying host.
> Who can appease her like a lover's ghost?
>   Who can avenge so well a leader's fall?
> What maid retrieve when man's flush'd hope is lost?
>   Who hangs so fiercely on the flying Gaul,
> Foiled by a woman's hand, before a battered wall?"

The following day William acknowledged his defeat, by asking permission to bury his dead; a favor which, for sufficient reasons, was not granted, the Irish most cheerfully agreeing to perform that last office for their enemies. Despairing of eventually capturing a place which even the women and children were resolved to defend to the death, he withdrew his guns, broke up camp, and marched his army northeastward, a sadder if not a wiser man. He shortly after took shipping from Duncannon, leaving Ireland for ever; and it would have been better for his reputation, if he never had visited it.

His entire loss in killed and wounded before Limerick is generally estimated at five thousand, including one thousand and sixty-two men and ninety-seven officers killed during the assault of the 27th of August, while that of the Irish on the occasion did not amount to half that number.

Thus ended the first siege of the "City of the Broken Treaty," broken, too, by the very man who was obliged to retreat ignominiously from its walls, and who, of all men, had the best reason to know, if not to appreciate, the bravery of its men and the devotion and heroism of its fair daughters. But the Prince of Orange was always cold-blooded, ungrateful; and his apotheosis may be fittingly left to the Orangemen, and such elaborate falsifiers as Macaulay.

The campaign of 1691 was again on the line of the Shannon, the Limerick garrison, after the retreat of William, having in great part made a junction with the troops at Galway and Athlone. This latter place, the "centre of Ireland," was besieged in the spring of that year by Baron Ginkle, commander-in-chief, and, after a protracted and gallant defence, taken by storm. Then followed the disaster of Aughrim, the death of St. Ruth, and the surrender of Galway through the treachery of O'Donnell and the treason of Lords Riverston and Daily. Sarsfield, who had been lately promoted major-general and created Earl of Lucan, Viscount Tully, and Baron of Rosberry, in reward for his gallant conduct in defence of Limerick, again threw himself into Limerick with seven regiments, resolved to defend it to the last, and, while waiting for French succors, to delay the enemy's advance by every possible means. On the eleventh of August, Tyrconnel died suddenly in a fit of apoplexy, and was succeeded by Lieutenant-General d' Ussan; and as Berwick had gone to France to hasten the supplies promised by Louis XIV, the burden of the defence fell upon Lucan. In the middle of the same month the Anglo-Dutch army appeared before the city, and on the thirtieth opened fire on the works. This time it was supported by twenty English armed ships, which had passed up the estuary of the Shannon and covered with their guns the south side of the city. The constant fire of this fleet and the land batteries soon reduced the town and its hastily reconstructed works to an undistinguishable heap of ruins: still Sarsfield's men presented so bold a front, and were so ready to meet any assault or make a rally, that the Dutch general feared to hazard a general attack, and even wrote to his master for reinforcements and supplies. But the days of Limerick's independence were numbered. Treason lurked in the patriots' camp, and several prominent Anglo-Irish officers of high rank, among whom was Brigadier Henry Lutterell, were discovered in correspondence with the enemy. Provisions, too, began to get short, and the ammunition was almost run out; the expected French supply not having arrived, though eagerly hoped for. Under these adverse circumstances, and overborne by the foreign officers, who were anxious to return home, and by some of the Irish bishops, who hoped for religious toleration of their flocks if Ginkle's terms were accepted, the heroic Sarsfield was reluctantly compelled to surrender the city, but still on terms which, if they had been faithfully kept by the English government, would have proved alike honorable to the soldiers and, comparatively speaking, very favorable to the Irish people.

In the Autumn of 1691, Lord Lucan passed to the continent with the remnant of the Irish army, and was commissioned by King James commander of his second troop of Irish Horse-Guards, in the service of France. In July, 1692, when the allies under William III were defeated at Clentirk by de Luxemburg, Sarsfield greatly distinguished himself, was complimented by that illustrious marshal, and appointed major-general by the French monarch. Again, in July of the following year, when de

Luxemburg at Landen gained a more decisive and glorious triumph over the usurper of James's throne and the implacable enemy of Ireland, Sarsfield, at the head of some French troops, part of Lieutenant-General Rubantel's command, was as usual remarkable for his desperate charges on the enemy's positions and for his uniform success. It was in the last of those charges, and in the very moment of victory, that he fell mortally wounded, a bullet having pierced his breast. While lying on the field, which his valor had so materially helped to win, he took in his hand some of the blood that flowed from his wound, and gazing at it for a while in silence, he mournfully exclaimed to those around him:—

"OH! THAT THIS HAD BEEN SHED FOR IRELAND."

SERGEANT COSTUME.

THE SIEGE OF ATHLONE.

In June, 1691, Baron Ginkle, commander-in-chief of the Williamite army, appeared before Athlone and summoned it to surrender. As it was garrisoned by the Irish troops, many of whom had seen the defeat of William and of this same Ginkle at Limerick, and were commanded by such officers as Sarsfield, O'Reilly, and Fitzgerald, it is unnecessary to record their answers. The Dutch general then proceeded to open fire on the works in the usual manner.

Those acquainted with the topography of Ireland are aware that Athlone is bisected by the Shannon, the portion on the Connaught side being known as Irishtown, and that on the eastern as Englishtown. At that time both parts were connected by a single stone bridge. After some days spent in cannonading, Ginkle resolved first to capture Englishtown, which, besides being weakly fortified, had only about four hundred defenders. The Franco-Irish generals preferred to make their grand stand on the west side of the river, as being a stronger position and in easy communication with their base of supplies. The preliminary bombardment having effected a breach in and early levelled the works of Englishtown, an attacking column of four thousand picked men were ordered to take it. This was easier said than done, though the assailants outnumbered their opponents just ten to one. Colonel Fitzgerald met the head of the column by a well-directed fire from his few pieces of artillery and a withering discharge of musketry; and then, ordering his little band to charge, gallantly repulsed the enemy. Again and again the attack was renewed and as bravely met, till Fitzgerald's men were reduced to a mere handful. Reinforcements were ordered up by Ginkle, and, overpowered by numbers, the few that were left of the Irish, after another desperate encounter, slowly and in good order retired, not, however, without destroying the arches of the bridge that connected the two parts of the town. We are not aware of any instance in history where a more gallant defence was made for so long a time by so small a body of men against such superior numbers of well appointed and veteran soldiers.

But an incident occurred shortly after which threw the heroism of Fitzgerald's men into the shade. In reading it, our thoughts are carried back to the traditional ages of antiquity, when courage in the service of one's country was placed first among the cardinal virtues. It happened this way :—

Ginkle, after taking the English town, erected his batteries there, and played with such effect on the works on the other side of the river that, on the twenty-eighth of June, he resolved to make an attack on the Irish stronghold. Under cover of his heavy fire, the broken arches of the bridge had been rendered passable by planks being laid over them, and as the Irish cannon had been dismounted and silenced, he ordered his troops to pass over and assail Irishtown. Sarsfield beheld the preparations for attack, but was powerless to prevent it, and so prepared as well as he could to meet it; but his arrangements, for that day at least, were premature. All the heroism in the Irish army was not confined to the commissioned officers. A sergeant named Costume, a corruption no doubt of some good old Gaelic name, saw a chance of assisting the general cause, and was quick enough to take advantage of it. As the soldiers of Ginkle were forming to cross the bridge, he volunteered his services to remove the planks, even in the very face of the enemy; ten others instantly joined him, and the devoted little squad, "the best eleven of Ireland," rushed forward and coolly commenced to pitch the planks and scantlings over the parapet. This manœuvre struck both sides with astonishment and admiration, but on the side of the Anglo-Dutch it was only momentary; for, opening upon the brave fellows, they swept the bridge with grape and solid shot and riddled the very planks with musket-balls. Nine of the eleven fell beneath the deadly shower, and but two escaped; but the work was done; and for that time, at least, Irishtown was safe from the embraces of William's hordes. History is silent as to whether Costume survived this heroic feat. We are inclined to think he did not, but let us hope that, in the future, "Ireland, a nation, will build him a tomb." In Greece or Rome, such bravery would have rendered his name immortal; in America, his memory would have been preserved in a thousand ways; but as he belonged to a persecuted race and a misrepresented country, few readers of modern times, except, perhaps, the curious students of antiquarian historical lore, have even heard or read of his name. As the great lyric poet has said of his country:—

"Unprized are her sons till they learn to betray;
Undistinguished they live, if they shame not their sires;
And the torch that would light them to dignity's way
Must be caught from the pyre where their country expires."

UNDRESS UNIFORM.

THE SURPRISE OF CREMONA.

In January, 1702, after a repulse by Prince Eugene, Marshal Villeroy, commander of the French forces in Italy, retired with his small army of five thousand men behind the fortifications of Cremona; his opponents, the Germans, also going into winter quarters between that city and Mantua, so as to watch both positions. But Eugene, one of the most skilful and energetic generals of his day, could not remain idle, and he resolved, with the assistance of some traitors within the walls, to surprise and capture Cremona. His plans were well and secretly laid, and their execution, up to a certain point, was carried out with great exactness and system.

The Po river flows by the walls of the city, and this was crossed at Firengola by

Prince Charles of Vaudemont with three thousand men, five hundred of whom were cavalry. His duty was to attack and carry the gate of the Po on the north side, as soon as the main body had entered the city by the opposite side. To effect this latter movement, eleven hundred men, under Count Kufstein, were introduced into the city by a long-unused aqueduct, who, on their entry, quickly secured a considerable portion of the rampart, while three hundred men were detailed to tear down the masonry which blockaded the gate of St. Margaret, and thus admit Eugene, Staremberg, and Commerci, with a force of seven thousand men. The instructions were carried out to the letter, and before the French had any intimation of the movement, the Germans were in possession of the great square and their cavalry were patrolling the streets, cutting down the French soldiers as they emerged in twos and threes from their quarters.

Villeroy, who was awakened by the unusual noise, arose, and hastily dressing himself, rushed into the street accompanied only, it is said, by a page. But meeting with a detachment of Imperial Cuirassiers, he was recognized and taken prisoner. His captor was a Captain McDonnell, an Irish officer in the Austrian service; and finding that he had fallen into the hands of one whom he believed to be a mere soldier of fortune, he attempted to regain his liberty by offering him the most tempting bribes. A large sum of money and the command of a regiment of horse are said to have been the inducements held out by Villeroy to the Captain; but, with true Irish fidelity and military honor, the offer was rejected, and McDonnell bore off his distinguished prisoner in triumph.

While Eugene was thus successful on his side, Vaudemont approached the Po gate, and Count Merci, who commanded the cavalry, assaulted it with his usual impetuosity. He was met by a withering fire from the guard, composed of only thirty-five Irish soldiers, who used their weapons with such effect that the whole of Merci's force were repulsed and obliged to skirt the ramparts, where, however, they discovered and captured a battery of French guns. This undoubtedly was the turning point of the engagement; for, if Vaudemont's force of three thousand had been able to pass in by this gate and form a junction with the main body, the gallant defenders would have been completely destroyed or captured—ground between the upper and nether millstones.

The little body of men who thus so materially contributed to change the fortunes of the day, was part of two Irish regiments then within the walls. Those were the regiments of Dillon of the old brigade, commanded on that occasion by Major O'Mahony, and the Athlone regiment of Colonel Burke, commanded by Lieutenant-Colonel Wauchop. Of the two commandants, the former, though inferior in rank, seems to have been the most conspicuous on that eventful day; the other having been wounded early in the affray. The first attack was made about three o'clock in the morning; and that vigilant officer, who had given orders the night previous for an early drill and parade, lay down in his clothes to rest. On the first alarm of danger he made his way to the barracks of the two regiments to arouse them from their slumbers, but, to his astonishment, and, no doubt, to his great satisfaction, he found them already forming in the street, fully armed and equipped, but with *no clothing on them but their shirts.* No time was to be lost; so, instantly leading them to the ramparts now in possession of Merci, he swept that general's forces before him and recaptured the cannon. Meanwhile, the Chevalier d'Estregue, with the regiment des Vaisseaux, and such other troops as he could rally, took post in a corner of the great square, and kept up a well-directed fire on the Imperialists, while Count Revel succeeded in capturing All-Saints Gate, though defeated in his attempt to retake that of St. Margaret. It was now ten o'clock, and the Irish troops had remained exposed for several hours to the inclemency of the weather in their night-shirts;

but the struggle is far from being over. Mahony is ordered to leave a portion of his men to defend the ground already rescued, and to make his way through the town to the Mantua gate, where the fight rages fiercest. The enemy's infantry opposes his march, but he drives them before him from street to street with little difficulty, but with considerable loss. At length, however, he meets a foeman worthy of his steel. A regiment of Imperial Cuirassiers led by Baron Freiberg dashes into his ranks, and a terrific combat between the unequally matched forces ensues. The numbers are on the side of his opponents, and his naked infantry have to oppose the steel-clad horsemen, then accounted the finest in Europe. The bold dash of the cavalry is met by the steady and well-directed fire of the Irish, again they rush in, and the fight becomes a general *melee;* the gleaming sabre is met by the bayonet, and horse and rider fall together. Many a saddle is emptied by the well-directed bullet, and when the quarters are too close for this, those gallant exiles spring on the animals and pull the riders to the ground. O'Mahony places his hand on Freiberg's bridle-rein, and tells him to ask for quarter; the German replies "no quarter to-day," and is instantly shot down by a private soldier.

Stunned but undismayed by the fall of their leader, the Cuirassiers attempt to rally for a last grand effort, but it is in vain; they only rush on the guns of the Irish to find instant death; and broken, decimated, and defeated, the small remnant left of the once splendid regiment wheels round and retreats with much more haste than they had advanced. Cremona is saved. Eugene retreats from the town. France is jubilant, and all Europe stands astonished at his defeat by so small a force of expatriated Irish soldiers. Louis XIV, as well he might, compliments the two regiments on their heroism, doubles the pay of the enlisted men, and promotes and rewards the officers.

The losses in this sharp and bloody affray were: in Burke's regiment, one officer and fifty-three privates killed, and thirteen officers and seventy-eight privates wounded; in Dillon's (Major O'Mahony), six officers and thirty-seven privates killed, and twenty-nine officers and sixty-six privates wounded; in prisoners, sixty-seven.

The desperate bravery of the Irish was never better illustrated than on this occasion; and as for their *coolness* under fire, there can be no second opinion, when we reflect that it happened in the depth of winter, and that their wardrobe was of the simplest and most primitive description. But lest we might be accused of too much national partiality, we will quote a short passage from Monsieur Voltaire, who, with the instinct of an atheist, and the vanity of the worse class of the Gauls, never had a good word for a Catholic, particularly if he hailed from the Island of Saints, when he could possibly avoid it. That sceptic, in his account of the surprise, says:—

"Officers and soldiers, pell-mell, some half armed, others almost naked, without direction, without order, fill the streets and public places. They fight in confusion, intrench themselves from street to street, from place to place. Two Irish regiments, which made part of the garrison, arrest the advance of the Imperialists. *Never town was surprised with more skill or defended with so much valor.* The garrison consisted of about five thousand men: Prince Eugene had not yet brought in more than four thousand.* A large detachment of his army was to arrive by the Po bridge; the measures were well taken, but another chance deranged all. The bridge over the Po, insufficiently guarded by about a hundred French [Irish] soldiers, was to have been seized by a body of German Cuirassiers, who, at the moment Prince Eugene was entering the town, were commanded to go and take possession of it. For this purpose, it was necessary that, having entered by the southern gate, they should instantly go outside the city in a northern direction by

* Voltaire's figures as to the strength of the garrison are nearly correct, but the force under Eugene is sadly underrated. The best historians place his troops within the walls at about eight thousand, independent of those under Count Merci.

the Po gate, and then hasten to the bridge. But, in going thither, the guide that led them was killed by a musket-ball fired from a window. The Cuirassiers take one street for another. In this short interval, the Irish spring forward to the gate of the Po; they fight and repulse the Cuirassiers. The Marquis de Praslin profits by the movement to cut down the bridge. The succor which the enemy counted on did not arrive, and the town is saved."

This description by the Franco-Swiss historian, it must be remarked, is far from covering the whole day's transactions, and is very incorrect, both as to the enemy's designs on the Po gate, and the method by which they were attempted to be carried out. It is inserted here mainly to show that the brilliant valor of our countrymen on that memorable occasion was so conspicuous, as to extort recognition even from their bitterest opponents.

Major O'Mahony, who so gallantly demeaned himself on this occasion, was, says the Abbé de Fairac, "appointed to carry to his most Christian Majesty an account of that memorable transaction, and performed that commission so much to his majesty's satisfaction that he granted him a brevet for colonel and gave him a pension of one thousand livres, besides one thousand louis-d'ors to defray the expenses of his journey to the court." The same impartial authority adds, in relation to this victory: "It must be said to the honor of the Irish, that this day was appointed by Providence to signalize their fidelity and undauntedness. The two regiments of that nation, which were in garrison at Cremona, made a most terrible fire on those who offered to approach near the post they had taken; and what is most singular in it is, that the officer who had taken the Marshal de Villeroy, going to them from Prince Eugene, to persuade them to surrender, they secured him; and so exasperated the prince that he sent Baron Frieberg, at the head of a great body of Cuirassiers, with orders to put them all to the sword, if they did not immediately surrender. That officer, having beheld many of his men killed about him, resolved rather to lose his own life in a fresh attack than to yield himself up to the Irish. His death daunted the Cuirassiers, who instantly turned their backs and fled; and their defeat snatched the victory out of the hands of the Imperialists."*

*. "History of the Revolutions in Spain." Translated. London: 1724.

CAPTAIN JAMES CANTILLON.

BATTLE OF MALPLAQUET.

The late Mr. John O'Connell, eldest son of Ireland's greatest agitator, many years ago employed a portion of his time in collecting materials for a history of the Irish brigades in foreign service, and in the course of his researches and inquiries he received from Le Baron Cantillon de Ballyheagen, Lieutenant-Colonel of the 3d Hussars and President of the Council of War in Paris in 1843, the following interesting communication:—

"A celebrated painter has reproduced in a picture, which is at present my property, an historical subject concerning my family and yours. It treats of my great grandfather, who was likewise the uncle of Mary O'Connell, the wife of Maurice, your granduncle. The subject is drawn from the archives of the Minister of War at Paris. This picture represents Captain James Cantillon at the battle of Malplaquet, in 1709, charging at the head of the grenadiers of the Irish regiment of Dorrington, the English troops commanded by the Duke of Marlborough. The official documents explain the subject of it in this manner:—When the left of the French army, taken in flank by the right wing of the enemy's army, under the orders of the Duke of Marlborough, began to recoil, the Maréchal de Villars brought up as quickly as possible the Irish brigade, which was in the centre. It attacked with fury the English troops, whom it repulsed. Cantillon, at the head of the grenadiers of the regiment of Dorrington, first approached the enemy's line, exclaiming to his men, '*Forward, brave Irishmen! Long live King James III and the King of France!*' He had his sword broken in the combat, and fell covered with wounds in the midst of the ranks of the English infantry, after having killed with his own hand an officer and several soldiers. There remained after the charge only fifteen men of the company of Cantillon; the others were stretched dead or wounded around their brave captain, whose glorious example they had followed. The painter has represented Cantillon, sword in hand, pointing out the enemy's troops to the Irish, and holding up his hat in his left hand, while exclaiming, 'Forward, brave Irishmen,' &c."

FIELD-MARSHAL COUNT PETER LACY.

HIS CAMPAIGNS AS COMMANDER-IN-CHIEF OF THE RUSSIAN FORCES.

The three most distinguished officers of the Irish brigades in France, and those who rose to supreme command and acquired a universal reputation, were the Duke of Berwick, and Counts Lally Tollendal and de Lacey or Lacy. The first was the celebrated James Fitz-James, an illegitimate son of James II by Arabella Churchill, sister to the Duke of Marlborough, who, notwithstanding the bar sinister on his escutcheon, was a man of excellent character and pure morals; the bearer of many titles and lordships, conferred for most valuable services in the field and cabinet, and the victor in many a hard-fought battle in France, Spain, and the Netherlands.

Thomas Arthur Lally Tollendal, who entered the service early in boyhood, of all the officers of Irish lineage who distinguished themselves on the eventful day of Fontenoy, was decidedly the most remarkable, whether we consider him as a soldier and a statesman, follow up his most eventful career, or sigh over his ill-deserved and most tragic death. Lally was the son of Sir Gerald Lally, or O'Mullally, of Tollendal, near the town of Tuam,* one of the original colonels of King James's army, and was born in Dauphine, France, in 1702, his mother being Maria Anne de Bressac, the daughter of a noble family of that province. At a very early age, he acquired a strong taste for military life, and developed a wonderful aptitude for mastering the most difficult studies of his future profession. While yet a child, he was frequently brought into the trenches by his father, a circumstance so far from discouraging the youth, that it increased his admiration for the life of a soldier. At the

* In Irish, *Tulagh-na-dala*.

age of twenty-six he was commissioned captain in Dillon's regiment, and promoted aid-major four years afterwards.

In the year 1732, he travelled through England, Ireland, and Scotland, with a view to ascertain the real strength of the Jacobin party in those countries, and returned full of zeal for the Stuarts' cause, and plans for a descent on the Irish or Scotch coast. In 1738 he was entrusted with an important and delicate mission to Russia by Cardinal de Fleury, and, though not fully successful on account of influences beyond his control, he received great praise at the French court, and deposited in the national archives two very valuable reports, one on the statistics of Russia, and the other on her gigantic designs and probable development. On the resumption of hostilities, we find him full major of Dillon's regiment and aid-major to the Duc de Noailles, a position which gave him control of the organization of the troops under that distinguished nobleman. He was present at Fontenoy with his regiment, and by his suggestions previous to the battle, and his bravery during the hottest part of it, contributed so materially to the defeat of the allies, that he was promoted brigadier-general on the field by Louis XV in person.

A most enthusiastic adherent of the Stuarts, he devoted all his remarkable powers of organization and diplomacy to originate and perfect the expedition to Scotland in 1745, in which so many of his brother-officers of the brigade were engaged, and which failed mainly because his instructions were not properly carried out. For his services in the royal cause he was created, by Prince Charles, Earl of Moenmoye, Viscount of Ballymote, and Baron of Tollendal. As quartermaster-general to Comte de Lowendhall, in 1747, he signalized himself at the defence of Antwerp, and in the battle of Laffeldt, at which latter place he was severely wounded.

In 1756, at the special request and urgent entreaty of the French East India Company, he was appointed by the king commander-in-chief of the French forces in the East, and sailed the following May from Brest with a force of about two thousand men, including his own Irish regiment, two men-of-war, and two millions in money, having previously been created lieutenant-general, commissioner for the king, syndic of the company, commander of the Order of St. Louis, and grand cross of that order. He landed with his force at Pondicherry, the company's principal stronghold on the Coromandel coast, in 1758, only to find its affairs in a hopeless state of bankruptcy, its officials lazy, ignorant, and utterly corrupt, its little army mutinous and demoralized, its scanty navy insubordinate, and, to crown all, the native princes, instigated and assisted by the English, everywhere hostile to French interests. With his usual energy and fertility of resources, he at once set to work to reform the abuses of the colony, and bring to terms by force or diplomacy the neighboring chiefs; but the evils had become so chronic, that even his great genius could not eradicate them. In vain he punished peculation and reproved neglect; in vain he performed prodigies of valor with his little army against Indians and English: he could not save a selfish and corrupt corporation foredoomed to destruction, and, in less than five years after his arrival, Pondicherry and its surroundings were in the hands of the British. Lally himself surrendered as a prisoner of war at the capture of Pondicherry, after having defended the place for several months with the tenacity and skill of a thorough soldier. He was sent to England, and thence to France, where new troubles awaited him. His severe and thoroughly honest administration in India had raised up against him a host of enemies among the company's officials and their friends at home, the most powerful of whom was the Duc de Choiseul, Minister of War and of Foreign Affairs. Through the intrigues of that unscrupulous minister, he was arrested, imprisoned, and tried on a series of absurd charges, including that of treason, and, having been found guilty after a mock trial, was beheaded on the 9th of May, 1766—twenty-one years after the battle of Fontenoy—in the sixty-fifth year of his age. This glaring act of injustice horrified both French and English, in fact, people of all nations, who had long admired him as a gallant soldier, a subtle and comprehensive statesman, and a gentleman of varied accomplishments and of the highest honor.

With the death of Lally, the Irish brigade gradually declined in numbers and importance, until eventually swallowed up in the chaos of the French Revolution.

But when we consider the magnitude of his commands, the unvarying success which attended his campaigns, the raw material he had to discipline and fight, and the absence of all family or national influence to aid his steps to promotion and fame, the greatest of those three illustrious captains was PETER LACY, born at Killeedy, in the county of Limerick, October 9th, 1678. Like Lally, he entered the army when very young, for we find him in his fourteenth year an ensign in the Prince of Wales's Irish regiment at the siege of Limerick.

After the surrender of that city he proceeded with his uncle, General John Lacy, to France, and entered the regiment of Athlone as lieutenant, in which capacity he served in Italy and on the Rhine, until, upon the consolidation of the brigade, consequent upon the peace of Ryswick, he was mustered out as supernumerary. Conscious, no doubt, of his innate ability, and ardent in the pursuit of fame, he proceeded to Hungary, then at war with the Turks; but shortly after his arrival the treaty of Carlowitz was signed, and he was again disappointed.

Peter the Great at this time requiring foreign officers to discipline his troops, Lacy became one of a hundred officers who volunteered for the service, and set out for Narva, where, upon his arrival, he was appointed captain in Bruce's regiment of infantry, in 1700. Here his brilliant career begins. Russia and Sweden were then at deadly feud, and Lacy's time was fully occupied fighting in the summer and organizing his command while in winter quarters.

His promotion was commensurate with his services. In 1703, he got a company of one hundred of the Russian *noblesse*, called the Grand Musketeers; in 1705, he was a major, and the next year a lieutenant-colonel and instructor of three regiments; early in 1708, he became colonel, and in the following December, at the head of three battalions of infantry, a company of grenadiers, a regiment of dragoons, and five hundred Cossacks, he attacked and captured Rumna, the headquarters of the army of Charles XII. For this exploit he was given the command of a regiment of grenadiers.

At the decisive battle of Pultowa, fought in the summer of 1709, he acted as brigadier under Bauer, and, though wounded, contributed materially, by his bravery and counsel, to the success of that day, which for ever broke the power of Sweden. "It was," says Ferrar, "Marshal Lacy who taught the Russians to beat the King of Sweden's army, and, from being the worst, to become some of the best soldiers in

Europe. The Russians had been used to fight in a very confused manner, and to discharge their musketry before they advanced sufficiently near the enemy to do execution. Before the famous battle of Pultowa in 1709, Marshal Lacy advised the Czar to send orders that every man should reserve his fire until he came within a few yards of the enemy. The consequence was that Charles XII was totally defeated, and in one action lost the advantage of nine glorious campaigns."

From this time till 1721, Lacy was actively engaged against the Turks and Swedes, becoming in succession brigadier and major-general in 1712, and lieutenant-general in 1720. With this latter rank, in the following year he made a descent on the Swedish coast, forced that government into the peace of Nystadt, and added to the Russian empire Livonia, Esthonia, Ingria, Corelia, and a number of Baltic islands. In 1723, he was in St. Petersburg a member of the College of War; and at the ceremonies incident to the coronation of Catharine I, he held the place of honor beside the empress's carriage; meanwhile being decorated with the insignia of the order of St. Alexander Newsky, promoted to be commander-in-chief of infantry, and assigned the command of all the forces around St. Petersburg and some of the provinces formerly wrested from Sweden. All this was accomplished before he had reached his forty-seventh year, and in a land which he had entered, twenty-five years previously, a stranger, unfriended and unknown, with nothing but his bright sword and keener wit by which to carve his way to fortune.

But greater honors were yet in store for him. In 1727, the illustrious Captain Maurice, Count de Saxe, who afterwards commanded as Marshal at Fontenoy, was elected Duke of Courtland. So famous a soldier, and a French one at that, was a dangerous neighbor for St. Petersburg; and Lacy was selected to expel him from the duchy, which he did with very little ceremony. In 1733, at the head of thirty thousand men, he marched into

Poland, and went through the same summary process for Stanislaus, who had been nominated king by a part of the Poles, and placed Augustus of Saxony on the throne. He took Warsaw and Dantzic, and fought several successful battles during the campaign of the next year, and received from Augustus as a token of appreciation a portrait of himself, set in diamonds, valued at twenty-five thousand crowns, and was dubbed knight of the White Eagle of Poland. In 1735, he terminated the civil war in that distracted country by the battle of Busawitza, where, with only fifteen hundred dragoons, eighty hussars, and five hundred Cossacks, he completely routed twenty thousand Stanislaites commanded by the palatine of Lublin.

France and Austria being then at war, he was ordered to reinforce the army of Prince Eugene with some ten thousand infantry; but shortly after reaching Manheim, the place of rendezvous, peace was declared between the belligerents. His army accordingly wintered in Bavaria, and he himself took occasion to visit Vienna. His own account of the results of this trip he notes in his journal, in the following few simple words: "I arrived there the 5th of February. On the 6th, I had a private interview of the Emperor and Empress, both of whom received me in a very gracious manner. On the 7th, I was also admitted to an audience of the Empress-Dowager Amelia; the 8th, with the Duke of Lorraine and the rest of the imperial family. On the 10th I was again admitted to an audience of the Emperor and Empress. The former deigned to present me with his portrait, richly set with diamonds, and also five thousand ducats in money. On the 11th I quitted Vienna; on the road I met a courier from St. Petersburg, who brought me the patent of field-marshal."

With the patent were orders for him to put himself at the head of his command and reduce the fortress of Azof, Russia and Turkey being again at war. He sat down before it in May, and in July it capitulated with its garrison of three thousand five hundred men, between two and three hundred pieces of artillery, and a large quantity of ammunition and equipments. Munich's army having lost largely in the Crimea, the residue was added to the command of Lacy, and he went into winter quarters at Karkow, to be ready for the opening of spring to make farther advances on the enemy.

Accordingly, in 1737, we find him in command of forty thousand men, supported in the sea of Azof by the fleet of Rear-Admiral Bredal, with instructions to invade the Crimea and subdue the Tartars. The Khan disputed his entry into that now peculiarly historical country, with a much superior force, and held the boundary line, that of Precop, a strong natural defence, in full confidence of being able to resist the invasion. Lacy, however, drove him from this position by a dexterous flank movement, and the Khan fell back to Arabat to endeavor to cover that stronghold. Major-General Baron Manstein, an officer who served under the Irish marshal for many years, thus relates in his memoirs the subsequent proceedings :—

"As soon as he heard that the Khan was arrived at Arabat, and that he was there waiting for him, he caused the depth of that arm of the sea, which separates this spot of land from the Crimea, to be sounded, and, having found a place for his purpose, he had rafts made, for the construction of which all the empty casks of the army and main timber-pieces of the *chevaux-de-frise* were employed; and by this means crossed this arm of sea, with the infantry and equipages. The dragoons, Cossacks or Calmucks, swam or forded it over. It had not been the Khan alone who had judged this a rash enterprise of the Marshal Lacy, when he marched on the spit of land towards Arabat, for the generals of his own army were of the same opinion. All of them except Spiegel waited on him one morning and represented to him that he was exposing the troops, and that they were all running the risk of perishing together. The marshal answered them that danger there was in all military enterprises, but that he did not see more in this one than in many others. However, he desired their counsel as to what they thought was best to be done. They replied, 'to return;' upon which Lacy rejoined that, since the generals had a mind to return, he would despatch them their passports for it; and actually called for his secretary, whom he ordered to make them out, and immediately to deliver them to them. He even commanded a party of two hundred dragoons to escort them to the Ukraine, there to await his return. It was three days before the generals could prevail on the marshal to relent and forgive them the presumption they had shown in proposing to him to retreat. The Khan, who imagined that he should beat the Russian army at the outlet near Arabat, was supremely surprised at learning that it had crossed the arm of the sea and was now in full march towards him. But he did not think fit to wait for it. He retreated towards the mountains, harassed by the

Cossacks and Calmucks close at his heels."

After some sharp engagements between the advanced guards of the Russians and the enemy, Karas-Bazar, one of the most important towns in the Crimea, was taken on July 25th, and, having been found deserted by the inhabitants, was burned to the ground. It contained about ten thousand houses, fifty water-mills, thirty-eight mosques, and two Greek churches. The day following, a battle took place between Lacy's command and the Tartars near the river Karas, which, though doubtful for a while, finally resulted in the complete defeat of the latter, with great loss in killed, wounded, and prisoners. Having fulfilled his mission, and destroyed more than one thousand fortified towns and open villages, the marshal took up a retrograde march, crossed the Russian frontier, and established his winter quarters along the Don and Donetz.

On the 6th of July, 1738, Lacy was with his army, some thirty-five or forty thousand strong, in sight of Precop. "The

Khan, with forty thousand of his troops, was behind the line where he hoped to render the entrance into the Crimea more difficult than it had been the preceding years. He had great confidence in the new lines, which the year before the Tartars had made before the Palus Mæotis. But Lacy disconcerted his project, and entered without the loss of a single man. For, in summer, the heats dry up a part of the Sea of Azof, and a west wind keeps back the flood, so that one may get into the Crimea almost dryshod. As good luck would have it, this wind began to blow, and the marshal lost not a moment in taking the benefit of it. He instantly drew up his army along the shore in a single line, and happily crossed the sea before the return of the flood. Some, indeed, of the carriages of the rear-guard, that could not come up quick enough, were lost by the wind having ceased to blow and the sea returning just as the army had passed. They seized upon a small fort called Czivas-Coula. On the 8th, the marshal marched towards Precop and sat down before it. The siege did not last but till the 12th. The continual fire kept up against the place, and the quantity of shells thrown into it, took great effect, and obliged the Turkish commandant to capitulate." In the town were found about one hundred brass cannon. The garrison, amounting to two thousand Janizaries, surrendered at discretion. Some days after, a sharp engagement took place between the Cossacks and dragoons and twenty thousand Tartar cavalry. The fight, though short, was desperate, and the enemy were defeated with the loss of over a thousand killed. Lacy then, —after razing the works around Precop, and finding it useless to advance farther into the interior, which from repeated incursions had become an uninhabited wilderness,— retired for the winter to the Ukraine.

This was his last active operation against the infidels, for he was recalled to St. Petersburg soon after and entrusted with a much more important duty. In 1741, war having been declared between Russia and Sweden, the marshal was sent with an army into

Swedish Finland early in September, and, with his usual rapidity, had in two days defeated the enemy under Wrangel in a decisive battle near Williamstrand, and stormed and taken that town with its guns, stores, and the remnant of the Swedish forces. Being late in the season, he recrossed the frontier and encamped along it for the winter. The news of this first successful blow of the war caused great rejoicing at the capital; and when Lacy, leaving his army in charge of his next in rank, visited the court, he was received with marked distinction. About this time, an incident occurred in the life of the marshal, which, but for his ready wit, smacking somewhat of his race and nation, might have been attended with very serious consequences. It is thus told by Baron Manstein:—"In December the revolution took place at St. Petersburg by which the Princess Elizabeth, the youngest daughter of Peter the Great, was made empress. Of the several secret arrangements for effecting this change in the government, it not having been thought advisable to consult Marshal Lacy, who never interfered with the intrigues of the court, he was applied to at three o'clock in the morning to say of what party he was,— that of the Grand-Duchess Anne, or the Princess Elizabeth? Although suddenly awakened out of sleep, perceiving that there *was* in fact an empress who had the reins, but not being equally satisfied if it were the grand-duchess or the princess who had succeeded, he replied: 'Of the party of the reigning empress.' At this answer, which discovered a quickness of conception and a great presence of mind, address, and judgment, he was conducted to court, that he might continue to enjoy his rank and offices, and even receive fresh marks of gratitude from the new empress."

In 1742, on Easter-Sunday, a sort of Know-Nothing riot took place in St. Petersburg, which at one time threatened the most serious results. The foreign officers, even of the highest rank, were insulted and outraged in the public streets; the appearance of a stranger was the signal for an assault; and, as many of the army in and around the city had joined the rioters, it was feared that it would be given over to plunder and destruction, if not speedily quieted. Lacy was called upon to execute this dangerous task, and he did so with his usual promptness and method; and thus, says a cotemporary writer, "saved St. Petersburg and, perhaps, the whole empire. Most certain it is, that, if it had not been for the good arrangements made by Marshal Lacy, the disorders would have multiplied and gone greater lengths."

This outbreak having been effectually repressed, Lacy in summer again invaded Swedish Finland with an army of twenty-five thousand men on land, and ten thousand on board the fleet which was to support him. He set out in June, and drove the enemy before him to the gates of Fredericksham, which they abandoned without firing a shot, but after destroying the greater portion of the town and the magazines, leaving, however, behind them in their haste one hundred and thirty pieces of artillery. On the tenth of July, the festival of St. Peter, the *Te Deum* was sung in the cathedral of St. Petersburg and all the principal cities of the empire, "in thanksgiving that the Russian army had taken Fredericksham, the only fortified town in all Swedish Finland, without losing a single man." The marshal remained two days near the desolated town, and then marched his army to the river Kymen, on the opposite side of which he beheld the whole Swedish army drawn up, with their guns in position, prepared to dispute his passage. A courier, too, had arrived from St. Petersburg with orders to Lacy not to pass the river, but to end the campaign by making it a fortified barrier against the enemy. The marshal, however, regarding neither friend nor foe, after advising with his principal subordinates, boldly crossed the Kymen, the Swedes retiring through Perinokirk, Borgo, and Helsingkirk on Helsingfort. Though these were all strong positions, the dexterity with which the Russian army was manœuvred kept the Swedes in constant dread of being outflanked and cut off from their base of supplies; and even at Helsingfort, the strongest of all, they did not feel safe, and were preparing to retreat to Abow, when Lacy, obtaining information of the movement, resolved by a counter move to defeat it, by passing his army through an intervening forest and taking possession of the high-road leading to Abow. "By four in the morning," says Manstein, "the whole army was under march and joinèd Lowendahl by six. Scarce was the junction made, when they saw the van of the Swedish army. The Swedes, terribly surprised at discovering the Russians in a part where they had by no means expected them, returned as fast as possible into their camp of Helsingfort, which they continued to fortify, and strengthened with a number of pieces of cannon."

They were, however, no match for the Russians led by such a soldier as Lacy; and in fifteen days they surrendered at discretion. "When the Swedish army capitulated it was near seventeen thousand strong, and all the Russian forces that Lacy had at that time under his command did not outnumber the enemy by five hundred. The garrisons of Fredericksham and Borgo, the various detachments that they had been obliged to make, and sickness, had reduced the Russian army to one-half; so that there were two-to-one odds that, if the Swedes had not submitted to those ignominious conditions and the marshal had attacked them, the Russians would have been beaten, taking into consideration the position of their camp, which they had had full time to fortify."* One of the fruits of this glorious victory was the acquisition of all Finland by Russia; and with it, practically and fitly, ends the military career of the great marshal, for the operations of the following year, though commenced on a grand scale and with great pomp, were not signalized by any engagement of moment.

On the 14th of May, 1743, the land forces and stores having been put aboard the galleys at St. Petersburg about to join

* Manstein.

the fleet at Cronstadt, "the empress went on board Marshal Lacy's galley, where she assisted at divine service, according to the Greek ritual; after which she made him a present of a ring of great value, and of a small golden cross, enclosing some relics; and embracing him, wished him a happy campaign. She then went to her palace, from the windows of which she saw the galleys move off in a line, giving her a royal salute as they passed." Her majesty, who seems to have taken the deepest interest in Lacy's movements, as she had the greatest confidence in his skill and judgment, also visited him at Cronstadt to bid him a parting farewell. However, the fleet of Admiral Gollowin, when ready to sail, was delayed for several days by foul weather; and when it did put out and came in view of the fleet of the enemy, that strict constructionist refused to engage it, alleging that, by an antiquated order of Peter the Great, he could not give battle except the odds of three to two were in his favor; and as the enemy's ships numbered twelve and he had *only* seventeen, he allowed them to escape unmolested! Lacy, disgusted and impatient at such imbecility, was preparing to land his forces on the Swedish coast when peace, on terms most advantageous to Russia, was proclaimed. As a mark of gratitude to the marshal for his eminent services in bringing about this great national triumph, the empress sent her own yacht to bring him back, so that he might participate in the general rejoicings and festivities with which the event was celebrated. Lacy soon retired to his estates in Livonia, where in his seventy-third year he died, having spent two-thirds of a long and eventful life in the service of his adopted country.

Some of the minor details of this short sketch of Field-Marshal Lacy we take from his own journal; but the authorities most relied on, particularly when an estimate of his character is formed, or a just tribute is paid to his great energy of character and profound knowledge of his profession, are General Baron Manstein's and the Prince de Ligue's military memoirs. But while we cannot but admire the genius displayed by Lacy, and his uninterrupted success in aggrandizing Russia, what must we think of the laws and the government that deprived his native country of the benefit of his transcendent abilities? The field-marshal, count, and commander-in-chief—the intimate of emperors and kings—in his own land, where his ancestors had lived from time immemorial, could not have held an ensign's commission! The repression of Irish intellect by the penal laws of England up to 1829, and since almost as effectually by national and religious prejudice, is one of the great evils resulting from the loss of Ireland's national independence; and it will be only when she regains that of which she is so unjustly deprived, that the world will be able to witness what a perennial spring of genius lies latent in the people of that gallant and unconquerable nation.

LIEUTENANT-GENERAL DANIEL O'MAHONY.

THE WARS OF THE SPANISH SUCCESSION.

The conflict for the throne of Spain between Charles, Archduke of Austria, and Philip V, the legitimate monarch, lasted from the beginning of the eighteenth century till A. D. 1714. The archduke's pretensions were sustained by the Germans, Dutch, English, Portuguese, and a portion of the rebellious Spaniards, particularly those of Catalonia; while Philip had only the aid of his loyal subjects, of France, and a portion of the invincible Irish brigade. Philip's commander-in-chief during the greater part of the war was Marshal Vendôme, and his opponent's troops were directed by the celebrated Prince Eugene. On both sides were many distinguished generals. Strange to say, the French contingent was commanded by an Englishman, the Duke of Berwick, natural son of James II, and the English, Dutch, and Portuguese by a Frenchman, Henri de Massue, Marquis de Ruvigny, created, by William III, Earl of Galway. The Irish troops which had been transferred by Louis XIV to the service of the King of Spain were under the immediate command of O'Mahony, the same who so distinguished himself at the surprise of Cremona, and who, after being breveted colonel by Louis, ennobled by James, and appointed governor of Brescello, in Italy, entered Spain in 1704 with the rank of brigadier-general.

With his usual activity, he went at once to work, and at the affair of Monsanto he not only saved the Spanish army in its retreat, but inflicted severe loss on the enemy, thus giving them a foretaste of what might be expected from the new element that had entered into King Philip's army. On that occasion "the *Sieur Mahoni*," as his contemporary French biographer calls him, "commanded on the right, when, towards evening, twenty Portuguese squadrons were seen, that, after remaining some time drawn up for action, opened to make room in the centre for their infantry, apparently amounting to sixteen battalions. They advanced with much confidence, as calculating, from the superiority of their numbers, on surrounding the Spanish troops and cutting them in pieces; they even took in flank and rear the dragoons and the regiments of the Queen of Milan and of Orders, which the Sieur de Mahoni, the Irish brigadier, commanded. But he received them with so much firmness and repulsed them with so much vigor, that he stopped them until he gained time for the rest of his troops to reach the defile on their left. When this was passed, he caused the regiment of the queen (Irish) to turn upon them and charge them so effectively that one of their regiments of dragoons, in a yellow uniform, which had likewise passed, was driven back again in confusion, leaving two hundred dead upon the place. This brought the enemy to a halt, till they could be joined by their infantry and artillery. Then the

Spanish troops retired in good order behind a ravine, the Sieur Mahoni repeatedly facing the enemy with his rear-guard and arresting their progress with the almost unceasing fire he kept up. Thus this retreat was accomplished without any greater loss than about fifty men, in the presence of a force three times more numerous."

In the Franco-Spanish campaign of 1705, we find at one time part of the garrison of Cadiz composed of the regiment "de Mahoni Irlandois," and again the ubiquitous chief, or, as an English historian styles him, "the famous Colonel Mahoni, who distinguished himself in so extraordinary a manner in driving the Germans out of Cremona," driving the adherents of the archduke out of Arragon. It may be here remarked that, though the French, Spanish, and even British writers have taken a great many liberties with the names of distinguished Irish soldiers who served on the continent of Europe during the last century, and tried as much as possible to bend them to conformity with the idiomatic sound of their respective languages, they were unanimous in according to those possessors of old Gaelic names the highest praise for fidelity to the causes which they espoused, for daring in their support, and irrepressible gallantry in their defence.

O'Mahony seems to have possessed not only military genius of a very high order, but wonderful decision of character and mental activity; and the war of succession, as it is called, gave him ample opportunities to develope and exercise those qualities. He was, in fact, constantly employed in active operations, and, like his countryman and contemporary, Lacy of Russia, his promotion and honors kept steady pace with his responsibilities. Accordingly, in 1706, we find him at the head of an independent command with the rank of major-general, having also been created by his grateful sovereign a Count of Castile. In the following year, he took part in the battle of Almanza, and, of course, contributed to that splendid victory, which has been justly said to have secured the throne of Spain to the Bourbons.

This important engagement took place on Easter Monday, 25th of April, 1707, near Almanza, in the province of Neurcia, and in decisiveness, and the character of the contending forces, was the precursor of Fontenoy. Though the numbers engaged were less, probably about thirty thousand on either side, the feelings and motives that actuated the combatants were precisely similar. On one side were French and Irish, with the addition of some Spaniards; on the other Dutch and English, supported by Portuguese. Early in the spring, the latter, under the command of Lord Galway and Das Minas, laid siege to Villena, while Berwick, who had been joined by O'Mahony, after scouring Valentia, was at Almanza. By a dexterous stratagem, in which two Irishmen of the rank of officers played a conspicuous part, the duke succeeded in drawing his adversary from his works, and forced him to accept battle on his own terms. The fight did not commence till three in the afternoon, but before nightfall the enemy was completely routed, leaving more than three thousand dead on the field, and four thousand prisoners in the hands of the victors, including about eight hundred commissioned officers. Twenty-four cannon and one hundred standards were also captured, besides a large quantity of military stores. The English officers alone, killed, wounded (including Galway), and taken in this glorious battle, amounted to three hundred and seventy-four.

The Irish troops engaged in this action consisted of one battalion of the regiment of Berwick, and four squadrons of O'Mahony. They formed a portion of the brigade of Maine, and the commander-in-chief, with a thorough knowledge of their temper and prowess, placed them against the English portion of the allies. When the final attack was made which decided the fortunes of the day, this brigade advanced, and when within thirty paces received the enemy's fire, but did not return it till within a few feet of their adversaries; " then," in the words of a contemporary English, and, of course, no friendly authority, "they charged them with fixed bayonets and threw them into such disorder that they gave way, without being able to rally, and, as in flying before this brigade, those battalions (five English) were obliged to pass a ravine, a great carnage of them then took place." Count O'Mahony greatly distinguished himself on this day, and according to the Chevalier de Bellevive, "performed, at the head of his Irish regiment of dragoons, astonishing actions," as did other expatriated officers like O'Dwyer, O'Carroll, O'Heffenan, &c.

Early in 1708 we find O'Mahony, now lieutenant-general, at the head of seven thousand troops, including three Irish corps, again in Valentia. Alcoy was taken by him on the 9th of January, and many other fortified places along the coast fell into his hands. In March of the same year, he sailed for Sicily with a considerable force, including his five hundred Irish cavalry, and remained there for nearly two years. His well-known efficiency as a commander, and his attractive manners as a gentleman, are admitted by the writers of those times to have been the chief means of retaining that island for Philip, when his other Italian possessions were overrun or lost by the disaffection of their inhabitants. In 1710 he was recalled to Spain, and during the summer campaign we find him with his usual vigor capturing fortresses, and, when enjoying a separate command, invariably successful. He had charge of the right wing of Philip's army at the disastrous battle of Saragossa, August 20th; and by his desperate and repeated charges on the overwhelming numbers of the enemy, not only secured the personal safety of that monarch when the day was lost, but covered the retreat of the defeated army. Again, in the following December, at a battle fought near the same place with better success (for Philip's army was this time commanded by Vendôme and not De Bay), O'Mahony was on the right, and there can be no doubt, from the statement of the king himself, contributed powerfully to the victory, at the moment the centre and left had given away and were about to retreat. "M. de Vendôme," wrote Philip, "seeing that our centre gave ground, and that our left of cavalry did not make any impression on the right, believed it was necessary to think of retiring towards Torrija, and gave the order for that purpose; but as soon as we were going there with a considerable portion of the troops, we were informed that the Marquis de Fal-de-Canas and Mahoni had charged the enemy's infantry with the cavalry which they had under their orders, and handled it very mightily, which caused us immediately to adopt the resolution of marching back with the rest of the army." O'Mahony followed up his success with his usual impetuosity, capturing men and supplies, and had not night fallen so opportunely for Staremberg, the Austrian commander, he would certainly have been captured by the intrepid Irishman. As it was, we are told that "the Count Mahoni acquired a great deal of glory on the battle-day of

Villaviciosa, at the head of the dragoons. The king was so satisfied with him, that he conferred upon him a commandership of the order of St. Jacques, producing a rent of fifteen thousand livres."

The following incident, which occurred at the battle of Villaviciosa, as related by the Chevalier de Bellerive, we transcribe from a very valuable work* recently published in Ireland, as an illustration of the spirit that animated our ancestors in those days, and the loyalty and devotion which they exhibited on all occasions towards the country of their adoption:—

"When the two armies were so near that almost every movement of each was perceptible, M. de Staremberg caused to be brought to his right wing a battery commanded by an officer wearing a red mantle and mounted upon a white horse,

---

* *History of the Irish Brigades in the service of France, &c. By John Cornelius O'Callaghan.* 1870. This immense compilation of facts, incidents, and dates, relating to the Irish soldiers in European service during the last century, forms a most valuable book, and should be read by every Irishman and descendant of an Irishman on this continent.

who let fly from the van into the regiment of Irish dragoons of my Lord Kilmaloc [Lord Kilmallock], which was upon our left, and which nearly closed it up. This regiment was not long without feeling the fire of that battery, the first ball killing a horse and then two dragoons. My Lord Kilmaloc, its colonel, being struck by a cannon-shot, one of his sons caused him to be carried to the rear of the regiment. The father, fixing his eyes upon him, said: 'My dear son, let me at least expire within your arms, since I have so short a time to live.' 'Father,' he replied to him, 'it is necessary for me to go where my duty and the service of Philip V summon me.' 'What! my dear son, you refuse me that consolation, and abandon me at the hour of death?' 'My dear father, I go to avenge it, or to find my own with the regiment.' The cannon-shot there fell like hail; the enemy themselves were surprised to see men so firm, so immovable and insensible to the terrible discharges of artillery, that they knew by that what was the courage and the intrepidity of those brave dragoons. * * * Although this regiment had been very much weakened during the cannonade from the right wing of M. de Staremberg, it did not cease to charge the enemy's troops with such impetuous ardor that they could not resist it. * * * The lieutenant-colonel of this regiment received a musket-shot through his body while charging the enemy, and the Marquis d'Ableville, one of its brave captains, sabre in hand, lost his life there, all covered with wounds, having won admiration by many brave and intrepid actions. The Chevalier de Heli [O'Healy], captain in the same regiment, distinguished himself in it, having had two horses killed under him by the enemy's cannon, and his brother, a cadet in his company, was slain there."

O'Mahony ended the campaign of this year by following up Staremberg, punishing his rear-guard, and capturing a number of prisoners, including one hundred and fifty officers; and the following season he had driven the enemy out of the greater part of Catalonia. Henceforth the war languished for want of organized opposition, and finally ended in 1714 by the complete and substantial triumph of Philip V, with whose success and the restoration of peace Count O'Mahony's career may be said to have ended—gloriously ended.

It is pleasant to recall the fact, alike honorable to Spain and Ireland, that the services of our countrymen in that long and doubtful war were, and have ever been, fully appreciated by that noble Iberian people; and that while the Irish brigade, formed during it, was long and carefully maintained, the surviving officers were treated with the greatest distinction, and they and their descendants admitted to the highest social, civil, and military positions. As one mark of his gratitude, Philip, by a royal declaration dated June 28th, 1721, placed the Irish Catholics resident in Spain on a footing of legal equality with his native-born subjects, an act which has ever since made the Spanish people friends with our countrymen.

CHEVALIER WOGAN.

STEALING A PRINCESS.

Cut off from all home ties, generally romantic and adventurous, and always brave and chivalrous, the life of an Irish officer of the eighteenth century was usually one of variety and change as well as of daring and danger. At one time fighting in the swamps of Holland, and at another reposing in the palaces of the Medicis, now suffering amid the snows of Finland, and next combating the infidel on the torrid soil of Africa, our exiled countrymen of that period must have thoroughly experienced the "spice of life," variety, in all its degrees of piquancy; and as their national character for adaptability to circumstances has been always the same, they must also have experienced a great many vicissitudes of fortune and achieved many strange actions, the accounts of which, in most instances, we regret to say, are lost or forgotten for ever.

There is one name, however, which stands out prominently in the annals of modern knight-errantry—that of Charles Wogan, whose authenticated adventures, alike honorable to himself, his country, and the cause he espoused, might well form the basis of many a thrilling tale and effective dramatic representation. Born at Rathcoffy, in Kildare, at a time when his creed and race were under the ban of alien invaders, he naturally sought distinction in foreign lands, and grew up a devout adherent of the Stuart cause. To a fine presence, a powerful constitution, and a natural aptitude for intrigue, he added the advantages of an excellent education, cultivated manners, and unflinching fidelity to principle, which afterwards made him the trusted agent of continental governments and the personal favorite of princes and monarchs.

The first public notice we find of Wogan is in England, in 1715, when an attempt was made to restore to the throne of that country James III, son of James II, for whom the Irish had suffered and lost so much. Young Wogan was deeply implicated in that attempt at restoration; was, in fact, one of the principal organizers of the "conspiracy," and among the first to take up arms in the cause of one whom he considered his legitimate sovereign. The attempt, however, failed, and on the surrender of Preston he was taken prisoner, sent in irons to London, and indicted for treason the following year. The trial, of course, it was expected would result in hanging.

A life so valuable should not have ended so soon and so ignominiously: at least so thought Wogan; for, with eight companions, he overpowered the guard, managed to escape from prison, and though a large reward was offered for his recapture, he, after many narrow escapes, succeeded in reaching the continent. His adroitness and daring appear to have captivated the heart of the son of King James, for when that prince, by the advice of his followers, as well as from his own inclination, resolved to offer his hand in marriage to the Princess Maria Clementina Sobieski, granddaughter of the most illustrious John Sobieski, formerly King of Poland, the future chevalier was appointed to conduct the delicate preliminary negotiations.

To us moderns and republicans, the union of even crowned heads does not seem a matter of much moment beyond the happiness of those directly concerned; but in Europe at that time, and previously, and even since, marriage, instead of being considered a sacrament and an affair purely domestic, was and still is looked upon as a matter of state policy, just as an armistice or a treaty is now regarded between two powers. The so-called "House of Hanover," the head of which was then reigning in England, was interested in preventing the "House of Stuart," represented in the person of the exiled James III, from forming an alliance with any family of distinction and influence on the continent; and being on good terms with Austria, the Emperor Charles VI was induced to imprison the Princess Maria and her mother, so as to prevent the proposed nuptials, a knowledge of which had been reached through the treachery or imprudence of some of James's followers. As long as the matter rested solely in the hands of Wogan, it was kept secret, and conducted with so much skill that a betrothal had actually taken place; but the folly of Murray and Hay for a time prevented its consummation, and led to the restraint put on the fair intended bride.

The place of confinement was Innsbruck, in the Tyrol, and the jailer was a General Heister. But James Francis Edward Stuart, though he could not regain his kingdom, resolved not to lose a wife, and so he determined to rescue his lady-love. Not in person, however—for it is seldom the nature of kings to court danger—but by deputy, and the vicarious honor was entrusted to Wogan. Now this was a sort of enterprise that just suited the temper and talents of the young Kildare man. He was ardently attached to the Stuarts, naturally hated the Hanoverians, revered the memory of Sobieski, but, above all, loved danger; and as there was every possibility that in case of failure his life would be forfeited, he resolved to obey his prince, and set free the lady.

This could not be done without assistance, and in so desperate a strait he naturally looked for allies in the brigade. In 1718–19, Dillon's regiment was in winter quarters at Scelstat, some miles from Strasburg, and thither, in March, the enterprising Wogan, after having had an interview with Louis Sobieski, father of the young captive, and obtained his consent to his plans, repaired to enlist recruits for their proper execution. He had many kinsmen, it seems, in the regiment, and this, besides the romance of the adventure, easily gained him adherents. Of the officers, however, he selected only three,—Major Richard Gaydon, and Captains Luke O'Toole and John Misset, the wife of the latter and her servant also accompanying the party. From an account of this escapade published in London a few years later (1722), it is stated that all this party, this forlorn hope, spoke French well, and that "O'Toole was master of high Dutch" besides. This latter fact has a comical significance when we consider that the gallant captain was noted even in his own regiment, in which were so many picked Irishmen, for his gigantic figure.

Provided with proper means of transportation, and furnished with passports obtained by Wogan, the rescuing force left Strasburg on the 16th April, and, after a week's travel without incident, arrived in the neighborhood of Innsbruck. By a well-devised scheme, the princess and her jewels were quietly taken out of prison at midnight, the servant of Madame Misset being left temporarily to answer in her place, and the little cavalcade set off at full speed for Italy, and entered Rome on the 15th of the following month, amid immense popular applause. The usual accidents of breaking down of carriages and want of relays, it is said, happened on the road, and much danger was apprehended from couriers who, as soon as the escape was known, were sent forward to apprise the authorities and cause their arrest; but as O'Toole and Misset brought up the rear-guard, it is scarcely necessary to say that the aforesaid couriers never overtook the main body of the enemy. It is even averred that these two Irish captains, having met by chance one of the messengers, treated him so hospitably that he was incapacitated from pursuing his journey for twenty-four hours, and when he recovered his senses he found that his kind entertainers had departed, and with them his despatches.

When the news of this desperate and daring adventure became public, it created a tremendous sensation in Europe. The Emperor Charles imprisoned or exiled every near relative of the liberated princess, and the "House of Hanover" set all its diplomatic agents at work to have her restored and her liberators disgraced and punished.

But all in vain. The young couple were married in the Eternal City on the 2d of September of the same year, and honors of every description were showered on Wogan and his companions. They were made Roman senators by patent from Pope Clement XI, and on the 15th of June, 1719, were admitted into the Roman senate, and, in the presence of a large multitude of enthusiastic admirers, were welcomed by the prince of that body, Count Hippolito Albani, in an elaborate and highly eulogistic speech. The prince, also, to whose arms they restored his betrothed, showed them every mark of favor possible under the circumstances, by knighting each, and conferring on them, according to their several degrees, higher ranks in his service.

Shortly after, Gaydon and O'Toole returned to Dillon's regiment, and no doubt the narration of their adventure enlivened many a mess and bivouac; while Misset and Wogan went to Spain and entered the military service of Philip V, where both rose to high commands, and obtained the rank of chevalier. In the history of that country in the last century, Wogan is mentioned as being in command of the Spanish troops in Barbary, and of having gained, in 1733, a very splendid victory over the Moors at Santa Cruz. He continued during a long life to enjoy the confidence of his adopted country, and was honored with many important commands by its successive rulers.

Like most of the distinguished Irish officers in foreign service at that day, he seems never to have lost sight of the interests of his motherland, and, while he remained faithful to the government and the people who had treated him with so much distinction, his thoughts were always turned towards the island he loved so well, and from which an alien and a hostile power had driven him, like many thousand other brave and intelligent men, and rendered them wanderers and outcasts on the face of the earth.

AN OLD-FASHIONED DUEL.

SWORDS FOR FOUR—COFFEE FOR TWO.

It was towards the latter end of Queen Anne's reign, when Mr. Mathew, the celebrated dispenser of Irish hospitality at Thomastown, in the county of Tipperary, returned to Dublin after his long residence abroad. At that time party spirit ran very high, but raged nowhere with such violence as in that city, insomuch that duels were every day fought there on that score. There happened to be, at that time, two gentlemen in London who valued themselves highly on their skill in fencing; the name of one was Pack, of the other Creed; the former a major, the latter a captain, in the army. Hearing of these daily exploits in Dublin, they resolved, like two knights-errant, to go over in quest of adventure. Upon inquiry, they learned that Mr.

Mathew, lately arrived from France, had the character of being one of the first swordsmen in Europe. Pack, rejoiced to find an antagonist worthy of him, resolved, the first opportunity, to pick a quarrel with him; and meeting him as he was carried along the streets in his chair, jostled the fore-chairman. Of this Mathew took no notice, as supposing it to be accidental. But Pack afterwards boasted of it in the public coffee-house, saying that he had puposely offered this insult to the gentleman, who had not the spirit to resent it. There happened to be present a particular friend of Mr. Mathew of the name of Macnamara, a man of tried courage, and reputed the best fencer in Ireland. He immediately took up the quarrel, and said he was sure Mr. Mathew did not suppose the affront intended, otherwise he would have chastised him on the spot; but if the major would let him know where he was to be found, he should be waited on immediately on his friend's return, who was to dine a little way out of town. The major said he should be at the tavern over the way, where he and his companions would wait their commands. Immediately on his arrival, Mathew, being made acquainted with what had passed, went from the coffee-house to the tavern, accompanied by Macnamara. Being shown into the room where the two gentlemen were, after having secured the door, without any expostulation, Mathew and Pack drew their swords; but Macnamara stopped them, saying he had something to propose before they proceeded to action. He said, in cases of this nature, he could never bear to be a cool spectator. "So, sir," addressing himself to Creed, "if you please, I shall have the honor of entertaining you in the same manner." Creed, who desired no better sport, made no other reply than that of instantly drawing his sword, and to work the four champions fell, with the same composure as if it were only a fencing-match with foils. The conflict was of some duration, and maintained with great obstinacy by the two officers, notwithstanding the great effusion of blood from the many wounds they had received. At length, quite exhausted, they both fell, and yielded the victory to the superior skill of their antagonists.

Upon this occasion Mathew gave a remarkable proof of the perfect composure of his mind during the action. Creed had fallen the first, upon which Pack exclaimed, "Ah, poor Creed! are you gone?" "Yes," said Mathew, very composedly, " and you shall instantly *pack after him,*" at the same time making a home-thrust quite through his body, which threw him to the ground. This was the more remarkable as he was never in his life, either before or after, known to have attempted a pun. The officers, though dangerously wounded, survived.

LORD CLARE.

BATTLE OF FONTENOY.

This great battle, the most decisive fought in Europe during the last century, was the one in which the heroism of the Irish troops in the service of France was displayed with the greatest lustre for themselves, the greatest advantage to the country that had given them a home—and to a certain extent, fame and honor—and, best of all, with the most tangible damage to the interests and power of the class that had been their greatest enemies at home and their most insidious maligners abroad. The particulars of this celebrated engagement have been so minutely described by contemporary historians, and are so generally known, forming as they have done the darling theme of many a song, tale, and oration, that it is not necessary to recall them here. We desire only to point out to the historical student the singular unanimity of all historians of that epoch—French, German, Irish, and English—in ascribing the victory of Louis XV mainly to the desperate and steady bravery of his Irish allies; though of course the writers of each nation looked upon the cause in which the opponents were engaged, the merits of the quarrel, and the results of the struggle, from a different stand-point.

With the people of Ireland, this grand battle has never ceased to be a topic of the greatest interest, and the success of the brigade in defeating England, a legacy of inestimable national value; and while they feel a conscious self-importance in referring to it, they have generally restrained their claim to recognition as the victors, or the countrymen of the victors, within reasonable bounds. The old apothegm, "the hour of victory is the hour of magnanimity," generally obtains with them,—we might say, too often for their own good; but as in this case the victory was so palpable, and the defeat so humiliating, we can afford to be generous, and in describing the gallantry of the Irish simply give a bald statement of the facts.

The eighteenth century was distinguished for what might be called its complicated wars. The one to which we now allude found England, Holland, Austria, and Hanover arrayed against France, who, single-handed, if we except her Swiss mercenaries and that ever-faithful force, always renewed, of the exiled Irish, not only defended herself, but carried the war into the enemy's camp. Early in 1745, the campaign opened in Flanders. The force opposed to the French in the field and fit for duty, is set down by all impartial historians at from fifty to fifty-six thousand men, including twenty-two thousand English and thirty-two thousand Dutch, Hanoverians, and Austrians. The whole were under the command of the Duke of Cumberland, of "bloody" memory, son to King George II, whose object was to relieve Tournay and eventually drive the French from the Low Countries. The French army, exclusive of those besieging Tournay and detached to defend the bridges over the Scheldt, numbered about forty thousand, including the Swiss guard and some artillerymen of that gallant little republic, and all the Irish forces then serving in France, viz.: the infantry regiments of Clare, Dillon, Bulkeley (Montcashel's formerly), Roth, Berwick, and Lally, and the cavalry regiment of Fitz-James.

Lieutenant-General Charles O'Brien, sixth Viscount Clare and ninth Earl of Thomond, commanded the Irish infantry on this occasion, and the celebrated Maurice, Count Saxe, the entire army— Louis XV and the Dauphin being on the field, and *ex-officio* commandants. The dissolute but fearless Duke de Richelieu figured as principal aid on the royal staff, and the amiable, enthusiastic, and astute Lally Tollendal spared all the time possible from his Irish regiment to inspect the night previous to the engagement, not only the French lines, but those of the enemy. As the result proved, his vigilance and foresight were, beyond doubt, among the chief causes of the final, and at one time unlooked for, results of the day.

On the morning of the 11th of May, 1745, after a heavy cannonade, the allies attacked the French position at Fontenoy in three columns. Their right, led by Brigadier Richard Ingoldsby, who was ordered to assault the redoubt at the edge of the wood of Du Barry, failed to perform this duty successfully, and remained comparatively inactive during the remainder of the engagement. The left, under Prince de Waldeck, though more fortunate, did not altogether succeed in breaking through from Fontenoy to St. Anthony; but the centre, a column of some fifteen or sixteen thousand men and twenty fieldpieces, led by Cumberland in person, penetrated the French lines, and for a while seemed to bear down all opposition. Marching in a solid column, firing with the steadiness and precision of trained veterans, and flanked by well-served artillery, they successfully routed all the French cavalry and infantry that essayed in vain to oppose their progress. Even the enfilading fire of the enemy's guns seemed to make little impression on their compact masses as they moved solidly on to assured victory. At this juncture, when the fate of nations hung suspended in the balance, the Irish brigade and two French regiments, that of *Normandie* and *des Vaesseaux*, which had formed the reserve, were ordered as a *dernier resort* to attack Cumberland's column, which had momentarily halted on the crest of a hill, preparatory to the grand *coup de grâce*. Promptly as the word was given, Lord Clare formed his men in line, having ordered them not to fire before charging, and, at the word of command, with the impetuosity of a whirlwind, the Irish troops swept up the hill, and in a very few moments the victorious legion that but lately was so certain of victory went down before the avenging steel of the exiles, or were fleeing over the adjacent hills, a scattered and disorganized rabble. Fifteen guns and two colors remained in the hands of the brigade. Its loss was, however, heavy, but in proportion to the fury of its onslaught. It amounted in officers killed or wounded to ninety-eight, with a proportionate number of common soldiers and non-commissioned officers. This victory of the Irish, so dearly purchased, but so nobly won, was the subject of warm congratulation by their countrymen and co-religionists throughout Europe, and created the greatest chagrin among their enemies, particularly in England. Louis XV and the Dauphin, who had been spectators of the scene, went in person to thank each of the successful regiments, and the historians and chroniclers of the day were unceasing in their praise of the brave *Irelandais*. Lally and other field-officers were promoted, pensions were liberally distributed to the wounded, and decorations to the deserving; while all that the second George of England could exclaim, on hearing the news of the defeat of his son, was, "Cursed be the laws which deprive me of such subjects,"— a sentiment which afterwards found an echo in the hearts of British statesmen, and doubtless, materially modified their views of the wisdom of penal laws and Catholic persecution.

CAPTAIN CAREW.

IMPLICIT OBEDIENCE.

Boswell, the biographer of the celebrated Dr. Johnson, and a Scotchman at that, relates the following incident of the war in Italy in 1765, in his "History of Corsica":—

"During the late war in Italy, at the siege of Tortona, the commander of the army which lay before the town ordered Carew, an Irish officer in the service of Naples, to advance with a detachment to a particular post. Having given his order, he whispered to Carew: 'Sir, I know you to be a gallant man. I have therefore put you on this duty. I tell you in confidence it is certain death for you all. I place you there to make the enemy spring a mine under you.' Carew made a bow to the general, and led on his men in silence to the dreadful post.

He there stood with an undaunted countenance, and having called to one of the soldiers for a draught of wine, 'Here,' said he, 'I drink to all those who bravely fall in battle!' Fortunately, at that instant Tortona capitulated, and Carew escaped. But he had thus a full opportunity of displaying a rare instance of intrepidity. It is with pleasure," adds the narrator, "that I record an anecdote so much to the honor of a gentleman of that nation upon which so many illiberal reflections are so often thrown by those of whom it little deserves them. Whatever may be the rough jokes of wealthy insolence, or the envious sarcasms of needy jealousy, the Irish have ever been, and will continue to be, highly regarded upon the continent."

MAJOR-GENERAL RICHARD MONTGOMERY.

THE INVASION OF CANADA.

General Richard Montgomery, the proto-martyr of the American revolution, was in his thirty-ninth year, having been born in the north of Ireland, A. D. 1737, when he was called upon by his adopted country to take up arms in defence of her new-born freedom. The choice was an excellent one, for, by temperament, education, training, and experience, he was eminently qualified to lead and govern men, even under the most trying circumstances.

At the early age of twenty-three, being then an inferior officer, he distinguished himself in the second siege of Louisburg; and, having been successively promoted to the rank of major and colonel, took a conspicuous part in the decisive battle between

Wolfe and Montcalm on the plains of Abraham and at the capture of Quebec. When the conquest of Canada by the British was complete, he returned home, where he spent some years with his friends and in travelling on the continent, but finally returned to America, settled at Rhinebeck, on the Hudson, in this State, and married a daughter of Chancellor Livingston.

His commission as brigadier-general was made out in June, 1775, and in accepting it he made use of the following noble and manly language:—"The Congress having done me the honor of electing me brigadier-general in their service," he wrote, "is an event which must put an end for a while, perhaps for ever, to the quiet scheme of life I had prescribed for myself; for, though entirely unexpected and undesired by me, the will of an oppressed people, compelled to choose between liberty and slavery, must be obeyed."

The design of Washington in invading Canada was to send two expeditions from separate points, which were to form a junction near Quebec, and, by a combined movement, to capture the fortress and city, then, as now, the most unassailable position on the continent, and at that time the principal stronghold of the English north of the St. Lawrence. One of those columns was placed under the charge of the infamous, but skilful, Benedict Arnold, who was to advance through New England and the eastern townships; and the other was to proceed from Fort Ticonderoga, and, after capturing the more western points, make a junction with Arnold's forces in the neighborhood of their main objective point. The latter was to have been led by Major-General Schuyler, but that officer falling sick, Montgomery took command. His march was rapid, his plans well laid, and his success, for a while, brilliant and complete. Fort Chambly surrendered to his attack, St. John's was taken, and Montreal soon after occupied by his troops; Canada, in fact, was more than half conquered, and all that remained was the fall of her last stronghold, Quebec. To effect this most desirable object, Montgomery, in November, notwithstanding the severity of a Canadian winter, put his force in motion, and after a toilsome and tedious march arrived in the vicinity of the city, and effected a junction with the other column, which had already arrived at the point agreed upon.

As might be expected, his own men had suffered much from the rigor of the climate at that season, but Arnold's men were even in a worse plight. However, on taking supreme command, for he outranked Arnold, he endeavored, like a good and humane general, to alleviate the sufferings of his soldiers, and by judicious words and example to inspire them with hope and confidence, and to infuse into them that spirit of patient endurance which is one of the noblest qualities of a military man, whether he be of the rank and file, or the commander of thousands. One who was present at his first review and inspection thus minutely describes the effect of his presence among the patriots:—" It was lowering and cold, but the appearance of the general here gave us warmth and animation. He was well-limbed, tall, and handsome, though his face was much pock-marked. His air and manner designated the real soldier. He made us a short but energetic speech, the burden of which was in applause of our spirit in crossing the wilderness; a hope that our perseverance in that spirit would continue; and a promise of warm clothing. The latter was a most comforting assurance. A few huzzas from our freezing bodies were returned to this address of the gallant hero. New life was infused into the whole corps."[*]

A month was occupied in preparations for the attack, and on the night of the last day of the year, so memorable in the annals of this country, it was resolved to make a simultaneous assault on the city and citadel from two opposite points. While the main body, under the commander-in-chief, was to attempt the Castle of St. Louis, the strongest and most dominant part of the works, Arnold was to enter the town by the suburb of St. Roque; a

---

[*] Mass. Hist. Collection, &c., vol. i.

point of rendezvous having been appointed inside, if both were successful, and a system of communication by rockets established. Arnold advanced his troops as directed, but on reaching the palace gate he fell seriously wounded, giving place to General Morgan, who penetrated some distance into the town, and held his ground in the street for a considerable time, till obliged to give way before superior numbers. His attack, however, was more in the nature of a diversion, and its ill success did not materially contribute to the disasters of the day. The principal duty of capturing the fortifications Montgomery reserved for himself, as being the most hazardous; those once taken, the city was at his mercy.

The Castle of St. Louis, and the other works which form the fortress of Quebec, stand on an eminence of about seven hundred feet in height, rising almost from the verge of the river at an angle of seventy-five or eighty degrees. At the base of this hill, and between it and the water, along what is called Diamond Cove, runs a road, the approach to which, on that occasion, was defended by an outwork mounting two guns, and was guarded by some militia. Montgomery advanced along this road from the west, and on the appearance of his advanced guard its defenders fled precipitately, but not before one of them, a New England sea-captain, it is said, touched off a gun, the discharge from which deprived the United Colonies of one of their best and purest officers, and killed or wounded several of his staff. It not yet being daylight, the cannon and small arms of the main works were turned in the direction of the sound of alarm created by the firing of the single piece of ordnance, with deadly effect; and having lost their leader, the Americans retreated in confusion. When the wintry sun rose late on the scene, the gallant Montgomery was found a frozen corpse, near the place of his former triumphs,—dead it is true, but fallen in a holier cause than that in which he had been formerly successful and had come out unscathed.

Such is the account given by Hawkins in his History of Quebec, and which has been generally received as correct; but there are other versions of the affair which differ materially from this, and, while they bear in themselves the intrinsic evidence of probability, are consonant with the traditions of the older inhabitants of the menaced city. According to these statements, Montgomery, following the river road until immediately beneath the Castle of St. Louis, faced his men to the left and ordered a charge on the works right up the steep face of the hill. While at their head, sword in hand, and in a small water-worn gully, he was mortally wounded by a stray shot from the garrison. The Irishmen of Quebec many years ago placed a painted board in this very gully to indicate the spot, and though frequently removed by the British sympathizers, it was as often replaced, until at length allowed to remain unmolested. In addition to the date, it bore the simple but emphatic words:

"HERE THE GALLANT MONTGOMERY FELL."

From a close inspection of the fortifications at this part of the defences, we are inclined to think that Hawkins is mistaken, as, from the nature of the ground, it would have been impossible to depress the heavy guns of the citadel sufficiently to cover the road leading to Cape Diamond within a mile at least of the works. However, as the time may not be far distant when some of our military countrymen may have an opportunity of critically examining the matter for themselves, we await their judgment with patience.

The body of the Irish-American hero fell into the hands of the enemy; and at first Sir Guy Carleton, the governor, with a petty spleen that became his position, and which has since been so thoroughly amplified in the person of Sir Hudson Lowe, refused his remains the poor courtesy of Christian burial. It was, however, at length conceded. In 1816, the Empire State, grateful to her adopted son, and proud of his heroism, caused his remains to be disinterred and brought to New York, where they now repose in the vaults of St. Paul's Church, at the corner of Broadway and Fulton Street, one of the most conspicuous parts of the greatest city of the New World. The marble slab, set into the wall of the church, bears the following inscription:—

THIS MONUMENT
WAS ERECTED BY ORDER OF CONGRESS,
25TH JANUARY, 1776,
TO TRANSMIT TO POSTERITY A GRATEFUL REMEMBRANCE
OF THE PATRIOTISM, CONDUCT, ENTERPRISE,
AND PERSEVERANCE OF
MAJOR-GENERAL RICHARD MONTGOMERY,
WHO, AFTER A SERIES OF SUCCESSES, AMIDST THE
MOST DISCOURAGING DIFFICULTIES,
FELL IN THE ATTACK ON QUEBEC, 31ST DECEMBER, 1775,
AGED 37 YEARS.

———

THE STATE OF NEW YORK CAUSED THE REMAINS
OF
MAJOR-GENERAL RICHARD MONTGOMERY
TO BE CONVEYED FROM QUEBEC
AND DEPOSITED BENEATH THIS MONUMENT,
THE 8TH DAY OF JULY, 1818.

It may be here mentioned that, on each side of the church, twin guardians, as it were, of their illustrious countryman's ashes, rise the obelisks of Thomas Addis Emmet and Dr. Thomas McNevin, who, though their advent in this country was later, equally, each in his own profession, "conferred honor on the land of his birth, and great benefits on the land of his adoption."

JOHN SULLIVAN.

HOW HE SEIZED AN OPPORTUNITY AND SOME CANNON.

When the news of the massacre of several citizens in the streets of Boston (one of whom, by the way, was an Irishman) reached New Hampshire, Major JOHN SULLIVAN and John Langdon, of Portsmouth, with a company of townsmen mostly Irish or of Irish descent, surprised the Fort at Newcastle, took prisoners the captain in charge and his small garrison, and appropriated for the use of the patriots one hundred barrels of powder, fifteen cannons, and all the muskets upon which they could lay hands. As the export of gunpowder to the colonies had been prohibited by the "mother country," this windfall was of great use to the minute-men of Massachusetts when they encountered the enemy in force at Bunker's, or rather Breed's, Hill, near Boston.

Sullivan of course accompanied his prizes, and took part in that initial battle of the Revolution, having in the meantime, for his timely services at Newcastle, been elected to the Continental Congress, and made a brigadier-general; and, when Warren was killed, and the patriots driven back and dispersed, he took command of them and reorganized their broken ranks. He was with Washington at the siege of Boston, and doubtless celebrated St. Patrick's Day, 1776, with all the honors, for on that day he had the satisfaction of seeing the English fleet sail out of Boston harbor with all the garrison on board, thus abandoning for ever the "Hub," which since has sadly forgotten the services rendered to it by such men as Sullivan and his compatriots.

Like his chief, Washington, Sullivan's subsequent career was honorable and consistent, and, if not always successful, it was by no means barren of good results to the struggling colonies. He commanded the American forces at the Battle of Brooklyn, or rather of Gowanus, and though assailed by a superior force and cut off from reinforcements by the interposition of the East River, then almost impassable, the disposition he made of his raw levies, and the persistency with which he maintained his position, elicited the thanks and praise of his commander-in-chief. Like Montgomery, Stark, and other expatriated Irishmen, he had learned the use of arms and the science of warfare in the Canadian wars, under British colors, only, as it would seem, to use that knowledge, when a fair opportunity presented itself, with deadly effect against the hereditary enemy of his race.

"MAD" ANTHONY WAYNE.

CAPTURE OF STONY POINT.

In the summer of 1775, several regiments were ordered to be raised in Pennsylvania and other States by Congress. In the former, amongst those commissioned as colonels, we find the following names of Irishmen: William Irving, William Thompson, Walter Stewart, Stephen Moylan, Richard Butler, and ANTHONY WAYNE. Of these the latter became the most distinguished, having earned a place in American history scarcely second to that of any of the partisan soldiers of the revolutionary war. For his gallant conduct in various engagements and skirmishes he was commissioned brigadier-general in February, 1777; and once in command of a brigade, it was rare to find him absent when any fighting was to be done. He was conspicuous at the battle of Germantown, and for his intrepidity and judgment at Monmouth he received the thanks both of Washington and Congress. During the dismal winter encampment at Valley Forge, during the darkest days of the Revolution, he may be said to have kept the troops alive, for he was a most persistent and successful forager. Disregarding all the comforts of life himself, he was ever mindful of the wants of others, and spared no pains to supply them.

His most brilliant achievement—one which, from its desperate nature and rapidity of execution, earned him the *sobriquet* of "Mad," as it was thought no sane man would have had courage to attempt it—was the storming of Stony Point, a post on the south side of the Hudson river, commanding what was called the King's Ferry, then the usual route of communication between the east and the States farther south. It also commanded the approach to the Highlands by the river, and may be compared, therefore, to a fort built at the junction of crossroads, facing towards the cardinal points of the compass. The position was a strong one, being protected by the river in front, and on both flanks, while a deep morass cut off all approach from the mainland. The garrison consisted of eight hundred men, and the supply of ordnance, ammunition, and small arms was unlimited, as the importance of the post demanded. About dark, on a quiet July night, Wayne noiselessly approached this formidable work, unheralded and unseen, and when close under its walls he gave the order for an assault, and his men went across the ditch and over the rampart with a celerity and impetuosity that was irresistible. "Mad" Anthony led them in person, and in ten minutes was master of the whole place—men, guns, powder, and shot. This was one of the most dashing and decisive engagements of the war.

That at Bergen Point, which occurred the following week, though perhaps not so daring, was equally successful, and fraught with great advantage to the American arms. The British were compelled to retreat across the Hudson to New York, and that part of Jersey at least was freed from a hostile force.

Many minor acts of General Wayne's career might be recorded, but his memory is so embalmed in the hearts of the American people, that it were useless to expatiate further on the prowess and daring of this remarkable Irish-American soldier.

GENERAL JOHN STARK.

BATTLE OF BENNINGTON.

The very name of Londonderry, N. H., suggests the birthplace of this distinguished soldier and ardent advocate of American independence. His early career, so characteristic of the future man, is succinctly told by Barstow in the History of New Hampshire. It is as follows:—" In this year (1753), a striking story is told of four hunters from Londonderry, who had wandered in quest of game into the territory of the Canadian Aroostooks. Two of them were scalped, and two taken prisoners. They were condemned at St. Francis to run the gauntlet. This consists in passing through two files of warriors, each of whom is privileged to give the prisoner a blow. The elder of the prisoners passed through first, and suffered little less than death.

The younger and remaining one was a lad of sixteen years. When his turn came, he marched forward with a bold air, snatched a club from the nearest Indian, and attacked the warriors as he advanced on the lines, dealing blows right and left with a merciless and almost deadly force. Nothing in the conduct of a prisoner so charms the savage mind as a haughty demeanor and contempt of death. The old men were amused and delighted; the young warriors, were struck with admiration at the gallant bearing of the youthful captive. They next ordered him to hoe corn. He cut it up by the roots, declaring that such work was fit for squaws, but unworthy of warriors. From that period he became their favorite. They adopted him as a son, and gave him the title of "young chief." They dressed him in the highest style of Indian splendor, and decorated him with *wampum* and silver. It was not long after this that Captain Stephens was despatched on an embassy to redeem the captives. The first one offered him was their favorite young chief.

Captain Stephens received him at their hands with delight. But no one of the rude warriors recognized in the young chief of their affection the future American general, JOHN STARK.

Stark had early taken service under the United Colonies, but, chagrined at finding officers much his juniors, and possessed of far less experience, he resigned his commission and retired into private life, in which course of action it may be said he followed the example of many brave and skilful men whom the shortsightedness of Congress, comprised almost exclusively of civilians, had driven from the army. However, when, on the failure of the attempt on Quebec, General Burgoyne advanced from Canada at the head of a considerable force with the intention of attacking New York, Stark's military ardor was again aroused. Burgoyne sent in advance a large party of cavalry, infantry, and artillery to forage in Vermont, and General Stark at the head of the New Hampshire militia prepared to dispute their passage. The opposing forces met at Bennington. The engagement lasted but a few minutes; it was short, sharp, and decisive, and ended with the total rout of the English, and the capture of guns, stores, colors, and munitions. This victory led to that of Saratoga, when the main body of the British surrendered; for, weakened by the destruction of so large a portion of his army and the loss of his guns, that unlucky general, Burgoyne, was unable to sustain a pitched battle, much less effect the main purpose of his expedition.

It was at Bennington, just before the fight, that the British commandant, Colonel Baum, addressed his troops in a grandiloquent oration, dwelling long on their duty to their sovereign, &c., &c. General Stark, who was a man of few words but of decisive action, also spoke to his men in the following laconic terms: "My boys, you see those *redcoats* yonder? They must fall into our hands in fifteen minutes, or Molly Stark will be a widow!" It is needless to say that Mrs. Stark was not a widow. The veteran himself lived to a good old age, and when, in the second war with England, General Hull ingloriously surrendered the guns he had captured at Bennington, no one regretted the mishap more than he,—in fact, despite his age and consequent infirmities, it was with difficulty he could be restrained from reëntering the service to avenge his country's defeat. Of such stern stuff were our Revolutionary ancestors made.

GENERAL EDWARD HAND.

HOW A DOCTOR KILLED HIS ENEMIES, INSTEAD OF HIS PATIENTS.

When a portion of the Irish Brigade in the service of France was sent first to the West Indies and then to Canada to assist in the defence of that colony against the English, one of the surgeons who accompanied the detachment was an Irishman named EDWARD HAND. When the treaty of 1763 transferred all that portion of the French possessions to England, Hand left the service, and settled in Pennsylvania. When the tocsin of revolutionary war was sounded throughout the land, the gallant doctor, throwing aside pill-box and scalpel, resolved to adopt the sabretache and sabre, and fight like a soldier in defence of the country that had given him a home and guaranteed him freedom. Like a true physician, he was fond of blood, but instead of killing off his friends *secundum artem*, he preferred to practise a little phlebotomy on the common enemy. Accordingly, we find him in the summer of 1775 a lieutenant-colonel in the regiment of his countryman, William Thompson, the next year a full colonel, and soon after a brigadier-general. Such rapid promotion of an officer who was a comparative stranger, without many friends, or any previous practical military experience, argues well for his capacity and bravery, and we are prepared for the eulogy of the historian who says that he subsequently "was distinguished in every action." He commanded at Albany in 1778, having succeeded General Sullivan, and that year made a successful excursion against the Five Indian Nations, who, through the machinations of Johnson, had taken up arms against the patriots, and greatly annoyed the outposts. In 1780 he got command of a light infantry corps and fought the Delawares, and in the following year he was commissioned adjutant-general, which position he held till the close of the war. He was a special favorite with Washington, and when that illustrious patriot consented to accept once more the office of commander-in-chief of the army, he advised the reappointment of Hand to the adjutant-generalship. This gallant officer died at Lancaster, Pennsylvania, in 1803, full of years and of both civic and military honors.

We seldom find gentlemen of the medical profession forsaking the healing art to deal hard and deadly blows, though in the Revolutionary times, when men's souls were stirred to their veriest depths, we have such instances as that of Warren, Hand, and some others; and even in these degenerate days we might mention some bright examples. We must not forget that, in one of the battles of our late civil war, we think at Gaines' Mills, June 1864, when Corcoran's Legion was hotly engaged, and a retreat seemed imminent, a regimental surgeon, Dr. Neallis, drew his fragile staff sword, and rushing into the midst of the partially disorganized troops, rallied them by his stentorian commands and undauntedly led them right against the enemy. Since then, he has been better known among the veterans of the Legion by the title of the "Fighting Doctor," than by the more peaceful one of surgeon.

COLONEL FITZGERALD.

THE BATTLE OF PRINCETON, N. J.

But little is known of this officer except that, like Lafayette, Colonel Stephen Moylan of Cork (afterwards in command of Moylan's Dragoons), and other distinguished foreigners, he served on Washington's staff and made one of his military family, enjoying not only the confidence and respect, but the friendship of the "Father of his country." The adopted son of Washington thus pleasantly alludes to an incident in Fitzgerald's military career: "Colonel Fitzgerald was an Irish officer in the old 'Blue and Buffs,' the first volunteer company raised in the South in the dawn of the Revolution, and commanded by Washington. In the campaign of 1778, and retreat through the Jerseys, Fitzgerald was appointed aide-de-camp to Washington. At the battle of Princeton occurred that touching scene, consecrated by history to everlasting remembrance. The American troops, worn down by hardship, exhausting marches, and want of food, on the fall of their leader, that brave old Scotchman, General Mercer, recoiled before the bayonets of the veteran foe. Washington spurred his horse into the interval between the hostile lines, reining up with the charger's head to the foe, and calling to his soldiers 'Will you give up your general to the enemy?' The appeal was not made in vain. The Americans faced about, and the arms were levelled on both sides—Washington between them—even as though he had been placed there as a target for both. It was at this moment that Fitzgerald returned from carrying an order to the rear; and here let us use the gallant veteran's own words. He said: 'On my return, I perceived the general immediately between our line and that of the enemy, both lines levelling for a decisive fire that was to decide the fortune of the day.

Instantly there was a roar of musketry followed by a shout. It was the shout of victory. On raising my eyes I discovered the enemy broken and flying, while, dimly, amid the glimpses of the smoke, was seen Washington alive and unharmed, waving his hat and cheering his comrades to the pursuit. I dashed my rowels into my charger's flanks and flew to his side, exclaiming, "Thank God! your Excellency is safe." I wept like a child for joy.'"

Looking back to the history of the American Revolution, one is astonished to find what a large portion of the armies of the young republic was made up of Irishmen and their sons, born on this soil, and it ought to be a source of deep gratification and honest pride to think that our countrymen and their descendants took so active a part in securing to posterity the liberties which we now enjoy. It has been calculated by the best authorities that the Irish element formed at least one-third of the officers and privates who took part in the great struggle from 1775 to 1782. We have mentioned above the names of only a few prominent officers of Irish birth; we might have sketched the career of many more of inferior grade, but even collectively they would be far outnumbered by those whose immediate ancestors were from the martial "Island of Saints." Then again there were a number of Franco-Irish officers who volunteered their services, such as McMahon, Dillon, Conway, and Roche Fermoy, who, ever anxious to have another blow at England, forsook the attractions of Paris and resigned the chances of promotion, to cross the Atlantic and place their swords and experience at the service of the Continental Congress. The Irishmen of to-day should feel deeply grateful to those heroic and liberty-loving men, for it was they who, by their fearlessness and public spirit, have given us the right to inherit the glories and fame of *our* "Revolutionary forefathers."

COMMODORE JOHN BARRY.

ORGANIZATION OF THE AMERICAN NAVY.

One of the greatest difficulties of the Continental Congress, once it had thrown down the gage of battle to England, was to establish a naval force which, if it could not compete with the dominant country, then, as now, the greatest maritime power in the world, might, at least, annoy her merchantmen, cut off her communications, and, in detail, capture her lighter-armed vessels. The colonists, from their frequent encounters with the Indians and French, were accustomed to the use of arms, and familiar with all the devices and "dodges" of warfare on land, but on the ocean they were perfectly helpless. England monopolized the carrying trade between the colonies and herself, and nearly every captain in her merchant navy was bound to her, not only by ties of self-interest, but by that prejudice against, and contempt for, the colonists, which first led to unjust taxation, and then to a long and inglorious war.

There were, however, some exceptions. Notably amongst them, was one John Barry, a native of the county of Wexford, in Ireland, who, at the breaking out of the Revolutionary war, was in command of the finest packet-ship that sailed across the Atlantic, to and from the American shores. Barry was born in 1745, of a race of sailors, and took to the water as naturally as would a young duck. At fifteen years of age, he entered the merchant service, and at twenty-three, he was captain of a full-rigged ship, the "Black Prince." While in this capacity, he met Washington at the house of a mutual friend, and, though neither at the time could possibly have foreseen the destiny in store for them, the acquaintance soon ripened into mutual respect and friendship. Towards the end of 1775, when Congress commenced to take active measures to form the nucleus of a national navy, it, doubtless at the suggestion of the general-in-chief, entrusted the execution of their project to Barry. A few merchantmen, then lying in the Delaware, were hastily fitted out as men-of-war, and the flag-ship, the "Lexington," was put under Barry's orders. To another, the "Alfred," the afterwards celebrated Paul Jones was assigned with the rank of lieutenant. The "Lexington" and the "Alfred" were the first two vessels that hoisted to the masthead the "Stars and Stripes" which has since been proudly borne over every known ocean, sea, and harbor, triumphant and unsullied.

Early in the following year, Barry was put in command of the frigate "Effingham," but, the Delaware being frozen solid, he had no opportunity to get to sea. In the meantime, however, he was not idle in the good cause; for, when he could not be of use in what may be called his native element, he took service on land, and, in the capacity of aid to General Cadwallader, did good service at the battle of Trenton. Though the British took advantage of the sudden breaking up of the ice, in the spring of 1777, Barry, by a system of naval guerilla warfare hitherto unknown, annoyed the enemy exceedingly, and, with his small craft and armed boats, captured many transports and supply-ships. For this effective service he received the marked thanks of Washington, and the title of Commodore from Congress. In the following year, he commanded the "Relief," but soon after he was ordered to the best vessel in the United States service, "The Alliance," in which he took the American agent to France, running the gauntlet through the English fleet, which was instructed to capture him, his ship, and the gentleman in his charge. On his return, he amused himself by capturing the "Atalanta" and Trespasa," in the same engagement. Though badly wounded in this fight, he refused to abandon the quarter-deck till his end was accomplished. In 1781, he brought the Marquis Lafayette and Count Noailles to France, and on his return by the West Indies, he was attacked simultaneously by three British frigates. Having been hailed by one of them, demanding the name of his ship, and that of the captain, he is said to have replied, with his usual *sang froid:* "The United States ship 'Alliance,' saucy Jack Barry, half Irishman, half Yankee:—who are you?" So effectually did he belabor those men-of-war, that they were glad to haul off in a very damaged condition, while he pursued his course to these shores without further molestation.

For twenty years after the war, until his death, in 1803, Commodore Barry was incessantly engaged in superintending the construction and equipment of the infant navy of America, but, more particularly, in training up a class of heroes who, in the subsequent wars of the United States, with France, Algiers, and England, in 1812–15, conferred the greatest lustre on the United States. McDonough, Boyle, Stewart, Decatur, and other distinguished officers of the navy, were his pupils; and it was from his success in educating them, as much as from his rank and subsequent scientific attainments, that he earned the proud title among his shipmates of "Father of the American Navy."

The adventures of Paul Jones, who, as we have seen, served as first lieutenant in Barry's little flotilla, are too popularly known to require mention here; but, while all credit should be given to that free-lance of the seas for his undaunted courage and wonderful tenacity of purpose, we must not forget that the crews with which he fought and conquered, were made up principally of Irishmen. In a Life of Daniel O'Connell, recently published, we find the following passage relative to the appearance of Jones off the Irish coast, and the effect it produced on the mind of the child, afterwards to be the great emancipator of the Catholics of Ireland, and the friend of civil and religious liberty in every part of the world:—

"When this daring adventurer encountered the British men-of-war," says the writer, "he laid himself alongside and sunk or plundered them in the open seas. Britain rarely encountered a more pertinacious and troublesome adversary than this hardy Scotchman, whose heroic intrepidity in the narrow seas, where he scared the British mariners, was only to be equalled by his gallantry in Parisian *salons*, where he delighted the French beauty, and was fêted, flattered, and lionized by the French *noblesse*. On the mind of the rosy child, Daniel O'Connell, then only three years old, this fierce rover of the surges made a fearful and ineffaceable impression. Gamboling at the head of Valentia harbor, that noble and capacious estuary, whose desolate waters, unbroken by a keel, were of themselves sufficient to inspire his imprisoned mind with aversion for the unnatural government which neglected it,—the comely and ingenuous boy, his golden ringlets playing in the wind, beheld with unspeakable interest three men-of-war one day looming in the distance or approaching the shore. These ships constituted the fleet of the privateer. They were commanded by the bold adventurer in person, manned, for the most part, by Irish seamen, and having a company of the Irish Brigade, serving as marines, on board. Paul Jones had swelled the number of his hands by drafts from French prisons, where many Irishmen captured in war were draining away their lives in dreary incarceration."*

But there were other Irishmen as well as Barry, McDonough, and Paul Jones's crews, wrestling with the common enemy of America and Ireland, on her own peculiar element. The first English ship captured in the Revolution was the store-ship "Margarita," which was taken in Machias bay, by the five hardy sons of Maurice O'Brien of Cork. Two armed vessels, the "Tapnaquish" and "Diligence," were sent in 1775 against the rebel village of Machias, but they also were captured; and when a squadron, consisting of a frigate, a corvette, and gun-brig, and several schooners, were despatched from Halifax to avenge the insult, the O'Briens, with their neighbors, drove

---

* Life and Times of Daniel O'Connell, &c., vol. i, pp. 19, 20.

it ingloriously back. "This affair," says Fennimore Cooper, in his "Naval History of the United States," "was the Lexington of the seas; for, like that celebrated conflict, it was the rising of the people against a regular force,—was characterized by a long chase, a bloody struggle, and a victory. It was also the first blow struck on the water after the war of the American Revolution had actually commenced."

Those O'Briens seem to have had the "strong weakness" of their race and country developed in a remarkable degree. Not satisfied with capturing the lighter craft, and repulsing the heavy-armed vessels of England, they each embarked in new enterprises; and, though some fell fighting for their adopted country, and others survived the conflict of battle, they were generally successful against the enemy, and always *sans peur et sans reproche*. Two McGees, Captains James and Bernard, also distinguished themselves on sea, during the Revolutionary war under the national flag, as well as many other gallant seamen of

Irish birth, whose names are now scarcely remembered.

Thus, ever, whether on land or sea, in charging on the enemy with the persuasive bayonet, or pouring in a logical broadside, the exiled Irish were found true and unflinching in their devotion to the land of their adoption, and consistently hostile to the power that drove them from their homes, endeavored to make their nationality and creed a mockery and a scoff, and themselves wanderers and outcasts on the face of the earth. This long unsettled account with England, they and we have been paying by instalments, on the continents of Europe and America: the final and last ought to be paid in Ireland, where the debt was originally created.

THE MEN OF '98.

THE WEXFORD INSURRECTION.

The county of Wexford, one of the thirty-two into which Ireland is divided, forms the southeast corner of the island, and is as remarkable for its topography as for the character and condition of its inhabitants. Bounded on the east and south by the sea, it is almost as effectually segregated on the west and north by two mountain-chains known in their respective parts as the Black Stairs and Mount Leinster, which separate it from the county of Carlow and the Croghan Mountains between it and Wicklow. It is thus formed by nature as a most favorable theatre for partisan warfare, and, except the line of the Shannon, presents the best *point d'appui* in the country for the operations of an invading or insurrectionary army.

The inhabitants are also a peculiar people, and, though each section of the county, north and south, differs essentially one from the other, they are just the people to fight, and fight desperately for their rights, when "patience ceases to be a virtue." The river Slaney divides the county into two unequal parts. On the right are Bargy Forth and some other baronies, the inhabitants of which are descended from Irish, Danes, Normans, and Welsh; and on the left are the celebrated Shilmaliers, of pure, unadulterated Gaelic blood. The first are of small, compact stature, frugal, industrious, and money-making, excellent farmers and close traders, not prone to anger or easily excited, but, when once aroused, difficult to be appeased or intimidated. Their neighbors, on the contrary, are stalwart, dashing, hospitable fellows; generous and lavish to a fault, for whom danger and even death, by sea or land, seem to have no terrors, but, on the contrary, a positive attraction.

Such were the people upon whom at the close of the last century the English officials in Ireland undertook to trample, and, for their own malign purpose, attempted to goad into premature revolt. To effect either or both objects, they had at their back as pliant, unscrupulous, and cruel a lot of tools as ever were handled by a despotic and usurping government. The legislative independence of the country having been wrung from England in 1782, the ministers of that power, upon recovering a little strength from a temporary cessation of hostilities abroad, set to work to undermine it, and not only to reduce the Irish Parliament to its former state of dependence on the "King and Council," but to destroy it altogether; a measure which they finally carried out eighteen years afterwards.

These attacks upon the Irish Parliament, covert and open, as well as the example of our American revolution, led to the formation of the secret society known as the United Irishmen, the ultimate object of which was complete separation from England. It at one time numbered about four hundred thousand members, and had its ramifications through all parts of the country; but strange to say, its principles and aims were less generally known or encouraged in the county of Wexford than in any other part of the country. In fact the peasantry and farmers, as well as those in a higher sphere of life, but of patriotic instincts, as a mass were ill-disposed to join an organization which required an oath of obedience to unknown and irresponsible persons; preferring to suffer the present evils in peace to encountering others of which they could form no clear conception, as long as they were allowed to pursue their ordinary occupations unmolested, and to worship their God undisturbed.

But they were allowed to do neither. It was not the design of the authorities that they should; and consequently the magistrates, the head of the different yeomanry corps, and the extra-loyal gentry, set to work to drive the people into armed opposition to the laws, such as they were. To prove their devotion to an alien government, they resolved to manufacture an insurrection, in the suppression of which they hoped to earn favor and patronage from the creatures of Pitt, enthroned in Dublin Castle. How well they succeeded, and how much blood and slaughter attended their efforts, we shall presently see. "At this period of confusion," says Hay, himself a "loyal gentleman," and an eye-witness of many of the horrible scenes that followed, "the first public intimation of disturbance in the county of Wexford was from a meeting of magistrates, held at Gorey on the 28th of November, 1797. There the proclaiming of sixteen parishes out of one hundred and forty-two, of which the county consists, was voted by a majority, of which my information does not afford me the number; but the measure was strongly opposed by eight of the magistrates present, including Lord Mountnorris, who must be naturally supposed to feel substantial reasons for his opposition to have the part of the county proclaimed wherein his property principally lay, and it is to be fairly presumed (whatever ground may be had by some reflecting people for thinking otherwise), that his lordship was not influenced, on this occasion at least, by motives of opposition to Lord Ely, his successful rival in the patronage of the county."* It was thus, and for such reasons, that the lives and liberty of the people were trifled with.

In consequence of this partial proclaiming, several persons were arrested and punished without any color of law, and informers began to rise in value. Still, the work did not progress fast enough; so, on the 25th of April in the year following, twenty-seven magistrates assembled at Gorey, and instead of sixteen parishes, proclaimed the whole county. "From this period forward," we still quote Hay, "many magistrates of the county made themselves conspicuous in practising the most summary means of quieting the county by the infliction of all kinds of torture. They seem indeed to have emulated, or rather rivalled,

* History of the Irish Insurrection of 1798, &c. By Edward Hay.

the conduct of the magistrates of the counties who had made trial of the *salutary* effects of persecution somewhat sooner.... They soon fell to burning houses wherein pikes or other offensive weapons were discovered, no matter how brought there. But they did not stop here, for the dwellings of suspected persons, and those from which any of the inhabitants were found to be absent at night, were also consumed. ... In Enniscorthy, Ross, and Gorey, several persons were not only put to the torture in the *usual* manner, but a greater number of houses were burnt, and measures of the strongest coercion were practised, although the people continued to flock to different magistrates for protection. Mr. Perry, of Inch, a Protestant gentleman, was seized on and brought a prisoner to Gorey, guarded by the North Cork militia; one of whom—the sergeant nicknamed *Tom the Devil*—gave him woeful experience of his ingenuity and adroitness at devising torment. As a specimen of his *savoir faire*, he cut off the hair of his head very closely, cut the sign of the cross from the front to the back, and transversely from ear to ear, still closer; and, probably a pitched cap not being in readiness, gunpowder was mixed through the hair, which was then set on fire, and the shocking process repeated until every atom of hair that remained could be easily pulled out by the roots; and still a burning candle was continually applied, until the entire was completely singed away, and the head left totally and miserably blistered! At Carnew, things were carried to still greater length; for, independent of burning, whipping, and torture in all shapes, on Friday, the 25th of May, twenty-eight prisoners were brought out of their place of confinement, and deliberately shot in a ball-alley, by the yeomen and a party of the Antrim militia; the infernal deed being sanctioned by the presence of their officers! Many of the men thus inhumanly butchered, had been confined on mere suspicion!!!"

But, as if such acts of barbarity were not considered sufficient to drive any human beings to desperation, a new element was introduced into the foul conspiracy. The North Cork militia, about four hundred in number, under the infamous Kingsborough, a second Kirke, were sent to the town of Wexford, and with them were brought the fooleries necessary to establish an Orange Lodge, the first ever known in that well-conditioned and peaceable city. This body had been recruited from the worst class of the community in the south of Ireland—Orange weavers from Bandon and the neighborhood, and the bastard sons of fathers just as illegitimate. They were cruel and cowardly, and it is hard to determine in which quality they most excelled, whether in running away at the slightest rumor of danger, or in butchering the weak and helpless, the defenceless woman or the puling babe. It is no exaggeration to say that their victims, during two or three months of the summer of 1798, must have numbered thousands, and their memory is as deeply execrated in Wexford to this day as it was three-quarters of a century ago. Beside them the Hessians were paragons of humanity and mercy.

The desired result at length came—an armed insurrection, but neither in the manner nor form expected. The miscreants of the North Cork militia and the pliant instruments of the so-called loyal magistrates were about to receive their first lesson. The men of Shilmalier tooks up arms, and resolved to suffer no longer the unheard-of tyranny of the magistrates and Orangemen. On Whitsunday, the 27th of April, Mr. Turner appeared in the town of Wexford with information that a rising had taken place, and that the indignant peasantry were assembled at Oulart Hill, a place about two miles from the town. Instantly every thing was in motion. The magnate of the English law had at length succeeded in rousing the people to action, and the North Cork, which had hitherto expended its renown in burning isolated chapels, and murdering in detail, now saw a hope of putting these devices into practice on a larger scale.

Accordingly, an expedition was fitted out

to massacre the men who dared to assemble at Oulart, consisting of cavalry under the command of Colonel Le Hunt, and a detachment of the valiant North Cork, numbering one hundred and ten men, under the charge of Colonel Foote. Loud were the boasts, and high were the hopes of this force when they left Wexford to disperse the ignorant rabble of Shilmalier, but they reckoned without their host. On coming in sight of the rebel position, the cavalry endeavored to take the insurgents in the rear so as to cut off their retreat, but, unfortunately for themselves, they were taken in front, and at the first fire totally demoralized, dispersed, and so frightened, that they never drew rein till they were again within the defences of Wexford. In the meanwhile the Orangemen of the North Cork, whose valor had been almost expended in burning chapels, and torturing the unoffending inhabitants in the vicinity of their posts, hesitated to attack the men on Oulart, however indifferently armed. Foote was in favor of retreating, but Major Lombard, who seems to have had some little courage left, advised an attack, alleging that the rebels "would fly at their approach." The attack was accordingly made. Two rounds were fired by the Orangemen, when, like a pent-up torrent that had at length burst its barrier, the Irish were upon them, and swept them away like so much drift-wood. Lombard the hero, Captain de Courcy, Lieutenants Williams, Warre, Barry, and Keogh, were killed, and "in short," says Hay, "*none escaped* except Colonel Foote, a sergeant (who mounted the major's horse), a drummer, and two privates"—five out of one hundred and ten! A more complete victory, considering the numbers engaged, we venture to say is not on the record of history. The insurgents had but five men killed and two wounded.

The defeated cavalry, as well as the other detachments which had been sent out to burn houses and slay the unresisting, retreated in consternation on Wexford, where a most ludicrous scene of panic and cowardice was exhibited. The Orangemen of the North Cork got under arms, and were actually *en route* to avenge the death of their comrades, when they were dissuaded from so rash a step "by some gentlemen." What were the arguments used we are not informed, but, from the previous and subsequent conduct of that organization, we are inclined to think that it did not require much logic or eloquence to deter them from confronting the victors of Oulart.

This fight took place on the 27th of May, and on the 28th the insurgents, flushed with victory, marched on Enniscorthy, then the second place in importance in the county. Their route lay by ruined chapels and burning houses, for it seems that the yeomen and militia cavalry had been out raiding the two previous days on their usual mission of fire and slaughter; all they met in colored clothes they deliberately murdered, and every house they came to they burned, in many cases with the inhabitants inside. Such sights were well calculated to arouse anew the indignation and vengeance of the people; and when they came in view of the town, it was resolved to assault and take it at all hazards. Enniscorthy was defended by part of the North Cork under Captain Soume, detachments of infantry commanded by Cornock and Pownden, and Ogle's and Richard's cavalry, all well armed, equipped, and supplied with ammunition. In this respect they had greatly the advantage of the insurgents, who had very little powder and only a few muskets and ducking-guns, their principal arms being rude pikes and stable-forks.

The assault lasted about four hours, and ended with the partial destruction and complete capture of the town. The rebels approached it, driving before them large herds of cattle, advice probably suggested by some classic philomath; and having almost surrounded it, they drove the enemy from street to street, and from one strong position to another until finally they were obliged to retreat pell-mell, and take the road to Wexford. "The military in their retreat," says Hay, "were very confused at first; however, self-preservation urged their keeping together, suggested by a private in the yeomanry. Officers had been induced to tear off their epaulets and every other mark that could distinguish them from the privates, considering themselves in more danger if they were recognized as officers."

The capture of Enniscorthy was a bold stroke, as it occupied a commanding position on the Slaney, and gave the insurgents undisturbed possession of Vinegar Hill, a prominent eminence in the neighborhood. The loss on the part of the assailants has not been accurately computed; but, of the defeated, a captain, two lieutenants, and nearly a hundred men fell before the fierce attacks of the half-armed Shilmaliers.

The news of the surrender of Enniscorthy added to the consternation of the Wexford garrison, now consisting of about fourteen hundred men, including two hundred citizen volunteers, with some pieces of artillery, and a plentiful supply of munitions of every description. The fact, also, that the massive old walls and castles by which the town was surrounded in ancient times, were, and are still, standing (except where thrown down to allow for the extension of streets to the newer parts of the city), rendered the positions almost impregnable to a tumultuous gathering of peasants without system, discipline, leader, or cannon. The cowardice of its defenders, however, particularly of the North Cork, who feared to meet the outraged people, even with all the advantages on their side, rendered all the natural defences of the place worthless.

Meanwhile many of the good people of the town, doubting the gallantry of their defenders, and fearing the wrath of the peasantry for their loyalty and adherence to the troops, hastened to pack up their effects and go aboard the vessels in the harbor, with the intention of escaping as soon as possible, while the Orangemen proposed as a necessary measure of defence that all the patriotic prisoners in the jail should be put to death! This proposal, though advocated even by many of their officers, was rejected by the majority from a wholesome dread of reprisals on the part of the rebels; and a couple of the most influential of the imprisoned gentlemen were temporarily liberated and sent to Vinegar Hill, to endeavor to induce the insurgents to disperse. This mission, however, had a contrary effect. They were, it is said, about to disperse, having, as they supposed, taught the government troops a salutary lesson; but the advent of envoys from Wexford, which had been considered too strong to be attacked, revealed to them the enemy's weakness. Instead of separating therefore, they immediately marched towards the town, retaining one messenger, and sending the other back to announce their intention of attacking the city itself.

This cartel, it may be supposed, did not tend to allay the fears of either the townsfolk or the garrison. The ships were brought into greater requisition than ever, the fortifications were strengthened, and the jail crowded with the suspected. An event which occurred on the 30th of May, did not diminish the general apprehension.

On the day previous, General Fawcett sallied out from the fort of Duncannon with the intention of reinforcing Wexford, having ordered his troops to follow, and getting as far as Taghmon, quietly went to bed, while waiting for his advanced guard to come up! The guard, consisting of Captain Adams and seventy men, and Lieutenant Burch with two howitzers, arrived there in the night, but not finding the general or the rest of the troops, kept on towards the menaced city. The insurgents in the meanwhile had marched from Enniscorthy, and taken post on the mountains of Forth at a place called Three Rocks, about three miles from Wexford, and commanding the approach to it from the southwest. Adams, on the morning of the 30th, advanced along the mountain road in ignorance of the rebel position, but he had scarcely come in sight of their pickets, when the main body was upon him, and a short, bloody, and decisive struggle ensued. His magazine was blown up, his guns captured, and himself and all his force destroyed, except one lieutenant and sixteen privates who were taken prisoners. Those "98 men," when in their senses, had a complete method of disposing of their enemies. Fawcett, and the remainder of his troops, which had marched on Taghmon the same day, on hearing of this disaster, hastily retreated to Duncannon, and did not feel himself safe till within its strong walls.

A sally was also made about the same time from the town by Colonel Watson, at the head of two hundred infantry and five cavalry corps, with no better success. They advanced within sight of the insurgents, when Watson, who it appears was no better general than Fawcett, advancing some distance before his men to reconnoitre, was shot dead by one of the rebel pickets. This was enough for his troops; they precipitately fell back on the town, where the news of all those reverses produced the greatest depression. We will let Mr. Hay, who was there at the time, and, though being a Catholic, always acted as a strong supporter of the government, describe the scenes that ensued:—

"A general and gloomy consternation now prevailed; every countenance appeared clouded and distrustful, and every person was circumspect how he spoke or acted, as all confidence was entirely done away, and each individual thought only of his own personal safety. Some yeomen and supplementaries, who during the whole of the morning had been stationed in the street, opposite the jail, were heard continually to threaten to put all the prisoners to death, which so roused the attention of the jailer to protect his charge, that he barricaded the door, and on hearing of a surrender, to manifest more strongly the sincerity of his intentions, he delivered up the key to Mr. Harvey. This gentleman was, indeed, so apprehensive of violence, that he had climbed up inside a chimney, where he had lain concealed a considerable time, when some gentlemen called upon him, but could not gain admittance until they gave the strongest assurances of their pacific intentions. Upon being admitted at length, they still found him up the chimney, and while so situated, entreated him to go out to the camp of the insurgents, and announce to them the surrender of the town, on condition that lives and properties should be spared. Mr. Harvey made answer, that as the insurgents on the Three Rocks were not from his neighborhood, and as he was not himself at all known to them, he imagined he could have no kind of influence with them; adding, they might possibly consider him even as an enemy. He was then requested to write to them, which he declared himself willing to do in any manner that might be judged most advisable. When he had thus consented, it became a task of no little difficulty to bring him out of his lurking-place, as in the descent his clothes were gathered up about his shoulders, so that it required good assistance to pull him out of the chimney by the heels. When he had arranged his apparel, and adjusted himself so as to put off the appearance of a chimney-sweeper, about two hours before the troops retreated from Wexford, Right Hon. George Ogle, captain of the Shilmalier infantry; Cornelius Grogan; John Grogan, captain of the Heathfield cavalry; James Boyd, captain of the Wexford cavalry; Solomon Richards, captain of the Enniscorthy cavalry; Isaac Cornock, captain of the Scarawalsh infantry; and Edward Turner of the Shilmalier cavalry—all magistrates—along with Lieutenant-Colonel Colville of the thirteenth regiment of foot, and Lieutenant-Colonel Foote of the North Cork militia, visited Mr. Harvey in the jail, and at their express request, he wrote the following notice to the insurgents on the mountain of Forth:—

"'I have been treated in prison with all possible humanity, and am now at liberty. I have procured the liberty of all the prisoners. If you pretend to Christian charity, do not commit massacre, or burn the property of the inhabitants, and spare your prisoners' lives.

"'B. B: HARVEY.

"'*Wednesday, 30th May,* 1798.'

"This note was undertaken to be forwarded by —— Doyle, a yeoman of the

Heathfield cavalry, who offered to volunteer on this hazardous service, when the proposal was made to his corps by Captain John Grogan. He had the precaution to put off his uniform, and to dress himself in colored clothes; but when ready to set off, he was discovered to be a Roman Catholic, and therefore reflected upon, for so the whisper went about, '*How could a papist be trusted?*' The yeoman, finding his zeal meet with a reception so contrary to his expectation, again put on his uniform and retreated with his captain; thus proving himself to the full as loyal as any of those who on the occasion displayed their illiberality, which even common policy, it might be well imagined, should repress at so critical a juncture. Dr. Jacob then proposed the enterprise to his corps, and Counsellor Richards, with his brother Mr. Loftus Richards, were appointed to go out to the Three Rocks on this expedition, to announce the surrender of the town to the insurgents, whose camp they reached in safety, though clad in full uniform.

Scarcely had these deputies set out upon their mission, when all the military corps, a part of one only excepted, made the best of their way out of the town. Every individual corps of them seemed to partake of a general panic, and set off whithersoever they imagined they could find safety, without even acquainting their neighbors on duty of their intentions. The principal inhabitants, whose services had been accepted of for the defence of the town, were mostly Catholics, and, according to the prevalent system, were subject to the greatest insults and reflections. They were also placed in front of the posts, and cautioned to behave well, or that death should be the consequence. Accordingly, persons were placed behind them to keep them to their duty, and these were so watchful of their charge, that they would not even permit them to turn about their heads; and yet these determined heroes were the very first to run off on the apprehended approach of real danger. Thus were the armed inhabitants left at their posts, abandoned by their officers, and actually ignorant of the flight of the soldiery, until the latter had been miles out of the town, and were therefore left no possible means of retreating. Lieutenant William Hughes of the Wexford infantry, with a few of his corps, was, it seems, the only part of the military left uninformed of the intended retreat, and this was owing to his being detached with these few yeomen to defend a distant part of the town-wall, and he and they were apprised of their situation, as were also the armed inhabitants, only by the approach of the insurgents; so that Mr. Hughes and his few yeomen, together with the armed inhabitants, are the only people that can be said not to have abandoned their posts in Wexford on this occasion. The confusion and dismay which prevailed were so great, as no kind of signal for retreat had been given, that officers and privates ran promiscuously through the town, threw off their uniforms, and hid themselves wherever they thought they could be best concealed. Some ran to the different quays, in expectation of finding boats to convey them off, and threw their arms and ammunition into the water. All such as could accomplish it embarked on board the vessels in the harbor, having previously turned their horses loose. Some ran to the jail to put themselves under the protection of Mr. Harvey. Officers, magistrates, and yeomen of every description thus severally endeavored to escape popular vengeance; and in the contrivance of changing apparel, as there was not a sufficiency of men's clothes at hand for all those who sought safety by this means, female attire was substituted for the purpose of disguise. In short, it is impossible that a greater appearance of confusion, tumult, or panic could be at all exhibited. The North Cork regiment, on quitting the barracks, set them on fire, which, however, was immediately put out. Lieutenants Bowen and Paye, with Ensign Harman, and some sergeants and privates of this regiment, remained in the town.

"It has been already observed, that thousands of people were seen to assemble during the entire morning, on a hill over Ferrybank, marching and countermarching in hostile appearance, and seemingly, waiting only for the moment that the town would be abandoned by the military, to take possession of it themselves; but their entrance, when this took place, was retarded, until boards were procured to supply the place of the flooring of the wooden bridge where it had been burnt. In the meantime, Messrs. Richards, after having run great risk, arrived at the camp at Three Rocks, and made known that they were deputed to inform the people that the town of Wexford would be surrendered to them on condition of sparing lives and properties: these terms would not be complied with, unless the arms and ammunition of the garrison were also surrendered. Mr. Loftus Richards was therefore detained as a hostage, and Counsellor Richards and Mr. Fitzgerald were sent back to the town, to settle and arrange the articles of capitulation; but these gentlemen, on their arrival, to their great astonishment, found the place abandoned by the military. The bridge being at this time nearly made passable, the vast concourse of people that had collected at the other side of the Slaney, was just ready to pour in and take unconditional possession of the town. It was therefore necessary to treat with these (it being yet unknown who they were), in order to prevent the mischiefs likely to ensue from such a tumultuary influx of people. Doctor Jacob, then mayor of the town and captain of the Wexford infantry, therefore entreated Mr. Fitzgerald to move towards the bridge, and announce to the people rushing in that the town was surrendered; and to use every other argument that his prudence might suggest, to make their entry as peaceable as possible. Mr. Fitzgerald complied; and instantly after this communication thousands of people poured into the town over the wooden bridge, shouting and exhibiting all marks of extravagant and victorious exultation. They first proceeded to the jail, released all the prisoners, and insisted that Mr. Harvey should become their commander. All the houses in town not abandoned by the inhabitants, now became decorated with green boughs, or green ornaments of one description or another. The doors were universally thrown open, and the most liberal offers made of spirits and drink of every kind, which, however, were not as freely accepted, until the persons offering had first drunk themselves, as a proof that the liquor was not poisoned, a report having prevailed to that effect; and which was productive of this good consequence, that it prevented rapid intoxication, and of course, in the beginning, lamentable excesses.

"The insurgents having now got complete possession of the town of Wexford, many persons who had been yeomen, after having thrown off their uniforms, affected a cordial welcome for them, and endeavored, by an exhibition of all the signs and emblems of the United Irishmen, to convince them of their sincere friendship; and it is indeed not a little remarkable, that many of those who, in this change of affairs, boldly marched out as occasion demanded, to meet the king's forces, now display themselves as stanch Orangemen of unimpeachable loyalty. Almost every person in the town threw open their doors with offers of refreshment and accommodation to the insurgents; and the few who did not, suffered by plunder, their substance being considered as enemy's property. Some of all descriptions, indeed, suffered in their property by plunder, on deserting their houses, and leaving none to protect or take care of them. The house of Captain Boyd was a singular exception. It was, though not deserted, pillaged, and exhibited marks of the hatred and vengeance of the people."

This cowardly abandonment of Wexford was witnessed by the insurgent army from their camp on the Three Rocks, which commands a very extensive view of the surrounding country, and the line of retreat was marked as usual with conflagrations and cruelty. The North Cork, as it was the first to run away, was, also, the most active in the diabolical work of death and destruction. We remember in our youth to have heard, on those same Three Rocks, the story of that day from a venerable farmer, who had, as he proudly said, borne the pike during that memorable period. He told us, when asked why he took part in the "rising," that from the spot on which we stood, he saw at one glance no less than seven chapels in flames fired by the runaway Orangemen.

Such sights naturally inflamed the minds of the already excited and now triumphant people, and rushing into Wexford, it was with great difficulty that they could be restrained from retaliating on the persons and property of such of the inhabitants as were known to have entertained and encouraged the miscreants who had deserted them. A few houses, indeed, were sacked, and three or four persons lost their lives in street broils; but, considering the greatness of the provocation, and the laxity of discipline among an unorganized mass of peasants and farmers, the forbearance and humanity displayed by them in their hour of victory, was wonderful. A regular system of order was introduced; posts, guards and patrols were established with an effort at military regularity, which shows that though without a leader or an officer of any actual experience, the natural aptitude for martial duties, which is so characteristic of the Irish, the most warlike people in Europe, renders them equal to almost any emergency.

The town was divided into wards, each of which had a company of armed men, under the command of the military governor, Captain Keough. Three old cannon were planted on the dilapidated fort of Roslare, commanding the entrance into the harbor, and an embryo navy in the shape of four oyster-boats, each containing twenty-five men, was established, and sent outside the bay to cruise for prizes. As Wexford has always been remarkable for her hardy seamen, this unique fleet was, for the time being, a complete success, and many captures useful to the insurgents were effected. Arms and powder were a great desideratum, for the supply was nearly exhausted, and only three small casks of the latter were found in the town upon its occupation. Efforts were therefore made to manufacture it, but, from want of proper materials, or defective skill, the attempt failed.

The town thus secured, and a permanent camp having been established at Vinegar Hill, as the most central point in the county, the army of Wexford, as it came to be called, after having compelled Beaucamp Bagnal Harvey, a very popular, but by no means revolutionary gentleman, to become their commander-in-chief, separated into two parts. One proceeded towards Taghmon, while the Shilmaliers set out for Gorey, on the north, in the neighborhood of which the yeomen and Orangemen had been perpetrating their accustomed atrocities. At their approach those gentry fled with all haste into the town, where it at first appeared that they would make a stand. Notwithstanding their numbers, however, before the insurgents had approached within sight, they incontinently fled to Arklow, in the adjoining county,—the North Cork under Lieutenant Swayne leading the retreat, of course.

On the 1st of June, this body and an independent band of insurgents met some reverses at Newtownbarry and Ballycanow, but nothing to dampen their ardor or check their progress. Gorey was evacuated by the royalists on the 28th of May, but, as the insurgents did not advance farther than the hill of Carrickgrew, it was reoccupied four days afterwards.

"On the 3d of June, General Loftus arrived there, with fifteen hundred men under his command, as did also Colonel Walpole, from Carnew, whence he had several times gone out to reconnoitre the camp at Carrickgrew. A determination was formed to attack this on the 4th, with the force then in Gorey, with which the troops from Carew and Newtownbarry were to coöperate, so as to engage the insurgents on all sides; and from these arrangements, and considering the force that was to act against them, little doubt was entertained of their total and speedy defeat. The army from Gorey marched out at the appointed time, and formed into two divisions; the one under General Loftus took the route towards Ballycanew, while the other, commanded by Colonel Walpole, proceeded by the Camolin road directly, to commence the concerted attack on Carrickgrew. The insurgents had, however, quitted this post, and were in full march towards Gorey, when they suddenly and unawares fell in with the military body under Colonel Walpole, at a place called Tubberneering.

"The meeting was equally unexpected on both sides; and this circumstance, no less true than extraordinary, neither party having scouts, produced an instantaneous and confused action, in which Colonel Walpole was killed, in a few minutes after its commencement, and his troops immediately gave way, and fled in the utmost precipitation and disorder, leaving the victors in possession of three pieces of cannon, two six-pounders, and another of inferior size. The fate of this action was so quickly decided, as to allow General Loftus not the smallest opportunity of affording the troops under Colonel Walpole any assistance. The loss of the military in killed and wounded was considerable, besides Captain M'Manus, Lieutenant Hogg, and Ensign Barry, of the Antrim militia, with many privates, taken prisoners. The rest in the greatest possible haste, being pursued by the insurgents, reached Gorey, which they as quickly passed through; but they would, in revenge, have put the prisoners in the town to death, had they not feared that the delay it would occasion might cost them too dearly. This account I have from a captain of yeomanry, who opposed with all his might the perpetration of such a cruel and barbarous deed, and who, to his honor, was incapable of countenancing such an atrocity under any circumstance. The retreat was thence very precipitate to Arklow, where a council of war was hastily held, at which it was as hastily determined to abandon that town, and this was accordingly put into execution. Some were so panic-struck, that they did not stop till they reached Dublin; but others stopped at different distances, when their horses or themselves were not able to proceed farther. General Loftus, on hearing the report of the cannon and other firearms in the engagement, not being able to go across the country, proceeded round by the road to the scene of action, where he found the bodies of many slain, and did not learn the fate of Colonel Walpole till he saw him stretched on the field of battle. He then moved towards Gorey, but thought it most prudent to alter his line of direction upon being saluted by the insurgents with the cannon they had just taken, and which they had drawn up to the summit of the hill of Gorey, which is immediately over the town, commanding it in every quarter. The general then marched to Carnew and from thence to Tulow, in the county of Carlow." *

The whole of the county of Wexford was now in possession of the insurgents,

* Hay's History.

except the fort of Duncannon and the town of New Ross on the Barrow river, and thither the column that had marched from Wexford to Taghmon and thence to Carrickbyrne, proceeded on the 4th of June, and halted at Corbet Hill, about a mile and a half outside the town. The garrison of Ross at this time consisted of over twelve hundred men, exclusive of the yeomen, all commanded by Major-General Johnson. To this officer, Bagnal Harvey, on the morning of the 5th, sent a written demand for the surrender of the place, but his messenger, as he approached the outposts of the royalists, was shot dead, which so excited the insurgents that, contrary to orders, one of the three parties who were to assail the town simultaneously, rushed forward, and, as might have been expected, was repulsed with severe loss, and so disheartened that it scattered in all directions, and prematurely spread the news of the defeat of the entire insurgent army. Thus the first attack was defeated through a want of discipline and obedience on the part of the men, and of determination and self-control on that of the persons acting as their officers,—defeats incident to all popular risings, but, in this case, fatal to the hopes and interests of the people's cause. The other columns assaulted the portions of the defences assigned to them with better success. They drove the enemy from the walls and ditches, resisted and defeated the 5th dragoons which charged them frequently, captured the Three-Bullet gate, cleared the streets, and finally forced the government troops over the bridge and across the river into the county of Kilkenny. But, unfortunately, what valor won was lost by misconduct. Instead of pursuing the enemy, they abandoned themselves to the pleasures of intoxication, and so, scattered and demoralized, they were driven out of the town in turn by the troops, who seeing their condition, rallied and recrossed the Barrow.

Stung by this defeat, the insurgents reformed, and again assailed the town, and this time the struggle was more desperate and prolonged. "The intrepidity of the insurgents," observes Hay, "was truly remarkable, as, notwithstanding the dreadful havoc made in their ranks by the artillery, they rushed up to the very mouths of the cannon, regardless of the numbers that were falling on all sides of them, and pushed forward with such impetuosity that they obliged the army to retire once more and leave the town to themselves." Undeterred by the lesson of the morning, no sooner had the enemy been driven out, than the former scenes of disorder and dissipation were repeated, and the consequence was that the army again reëntered, and the insurgents were a second time compelled to fall back. A third attempt was made to win the prize they had twice so heedlessly lost, but in vain; they were defeated with great loss and obliged to retreat to Carrickbyrne. Their total loss on this day could not have been less than one thousand, while that of the troops is set down at two hundred and thirty, including Lord Mountjoy, colonel of the Dublin militia, and several officers of rank. Among the insurgents, the principal one who fell was John Kielly of Killean, an enthusiastic, intelligent, and gallant patriot.

The battle of Ross was the turning point in the insurrection; and though successful in several subsequent skirmishes, the fortunes of the insurgents waned, and finally died out in blood and terror. Had they but been as prudent as brave, and held the town when in their power, there can be no doubt that the people of the neighboring counties would have taken up arms *en masse*; in fact, in Kilkenny, Carlow, and Wicklow, they had partially done so, and the insurrection would have become general at least in the south and southeast of Ireland. But the defeat at Ross intimidated the adjoining counties; and Wexford left to herself, was soon surrounded by at least twenty thousand government troops, which there was no necessity for employing elsewhere. The repulse at Arklow on the 9th of June, the retreat from Lacken Hill on the

19th, the disaster at Fook's Mill the day following, and the battle of Enniscorthy on the 21st, may be said to have closed the "rebellion" in that part of the island. Some of the insurgents found their way into Carlow, Kilkenny, Wicklow, and Meath, still fighting to the last, but with no other end or object than to avoid the scaffold and sell their lives as dearly as possible, till worn out and exhausted, the remnant surrendered to General Dundas, on condition that they and their leaders should be at liberty "to retire whither they pleased outside the British dominions."

We pass over in silence the scenes of rapine, bloodshed, and judicial murder, which followed the reëstablishment of the English power in that devoted county, as too horrible even for contemplation. Such unheard-of cruelty, such unmitigated acts of barbarity as were practised by the judges, officers, yeomen, Orangemen, and Hessians, are without a parallel in the annals of any other country in Christendom, save, perhaps, in Ireland herself in the days of Elizabeth and Cromwell. Even the French Revolution does not afford such instances of coarse, brutal, and demoniacal ferocity. Innocent and guilty, youth and age, delicate women and robust men, priest and peasant,— all suffered and were tortured alike. In glancing over this period we have quoted largely from *Hay's History;* not only because his is the most impartial narrative of the dire events of '98 written, but, as he was personally cognizant of most of the doings on both sides, and withal well affected to the government of the day, he cannot be accused of partiality to the people. His statements of the conduct of the courts-martial established to try the insurgents, and of the acts of wholly unauthorized individuals, are simply revolting. Even the Rev. Mr. Gordon, a Protestant, whose animus may be judged by the terms he employs, is forced to acknowledge some cases of rank injustice. Of the trial and execution of Father Redmond, whose only offence was that he tried to save Lord Mountnorris's house from pillage, he says:—

"Of the rebellious conduct of Redmond, coadjutor to Father Francis Kavanagh, in the parish of Clough, of which I was twenty-three years curate, I can find no other proof than the sentence of the court-martial which consigned him to death. He was accused by the Earl of Mountnorris of having appeared as chief among a party of rebels who committed some depredations at his lordship's house, while he alleged that his object in appearing on the occasion was, to endeavor to prevent the plundering of the house, in which he had partly succeeded. Coming into Gorey on a message from the earl, seemingly unconscious of guilt, he was treated as if manifestly guilty before trial—knocked down in the street, and rudely dragged by some yeomen. I mean not to arraign the justice of the noble lord, his prosecutor, nor the members of the court-martial. The former, who had rendered himself in no small degree responsible for the loyalty of the Wexfordian Romanists,, had doubtless good reasons for his conduct; and the latter could have no personal animosity against the accused, nor other unfavorable bias than what naturally arose from the turbid state of affairs, when accusation against a Romish priest was considered as a strong presumption of guilt. But his Protestant neighbors who had not been able to escape from the rebels, assured me that, while the latter were in possession of the country, he was constantly hiding in Protestant houses from the rebels, and that many Romanists expressed great resentment against him as a traitor to their cause. That he expected not the rebellion to be successful, appears from this, that, when the wife of Nathaniel Stedman (one of my Protestant parishioners) applied to him to baptize her child, he told her that he acceded to her request, merely lest the child should die unbaptized, in the necessary absence of her minister, on condition that she should promise to make the proper apology for him to me on my return to the parish."*

Alluding to this case, Hay adds:—" It

* Gordon's History of the Irish Rebellion, pp. 185, 186.

is a melancholy reflection to think how many innocent persons were condemned. I have heard of numbers, of whose innocence the smallest doubt cannot be entertained, whose conduct merited reward instead of punishment; yet they fell victims to the purest sentiments of philanthropy, which dictated their interference: these have been perverted by their enemies, who are also those of the human race, into crimes utterly unpardonable. Is this any thing less than arraigning benevolence and humanity, the most amiable qualities of the soul of man, as criminal and atrocious? But every man's breast, whatever be his principles, will tell him with irresistible force, that crime and atrocity lie at the other side. From personal knowledge of the circumstances, I knew five or six who were innocent of the charges and of the deeds sworn against them, and who still were condemned and executed. In these turbid and distracted times, I have seen persons sunk so much below the level of human nature, that I do believe they were not capable of judgment or recollection; which accounts to me in some degree for the various assertions, even testimonies on trials, and affidavits made by different persons, who might as well relate their dreams for facts. The dreadful prejudice, hateful as uncharitable, entertained against Catholics, has also occasioned the death of many; and the general excuse and impunity of Protestants, who joined in the insurrection, have induced many to avail themselves of this favorable circumstance to change with the times; and to testify their loyalty, they accuse the very persons they themselves seduced to join the association of United Irishmen, and thus cut off all the existing proof of their own delinquency by a consummation of villany."

This year and the two succeeding were marked by scores of summary executions; hundreds were doomed to servitude, to waste their lives in the company of felons far from the land they loved so well, while many, who were induced to enter the English army to save their lives and liberty, fell on the sands of Egypt fighting under Abercrombie, in defence of that flag which had ever been to them the emblem of persecution and tyranny.

There is, however, a moral to be learned from every calamity, national as well as personal; and in this case it is, that even Irish bravery, undisciplined, unofficered, and devoid of the proper munitions of regular warfare, is no match for organized and abundantly supplied forces, such as England is always able to command. The people of Wexford, it is true, did wonders in a short time, and, had the whole of the country risen simultaneously in armed revolt, and exhibited equal daring and perseverance, the power of Great Britain would have been seriously jeopardized; but, even then, it is very doubtful if a successful revolution would have crowned their efforts. Warfare is a science not to be learned in a day or a week, and each successive war demonstrates the fact that victory generally inclines, if not to the side of the "heavy artillery," at least to that which has the best commissariat, the truest guns, and the largest supply of arms of precision. Let those who talk so glibly of freeing Ireland by force remember this, and profit by the lesson it teaches before exposing their chivalrous country to the tender mercies of English law and English treachery.

GENERAL COUNT O'CONNELL.

LAST DAYS OF THE IRISH BRIGADE IN FRANCE.

In 1792, the survivors of the celebrated Irish Brigade, which had served for a full century in the armies of France with such renown and fidelity, quitted the soil of that country for ever. The occasion was one of deep melancholy and regret, both on the side of the veteran soldiers, and the royal family whose interests they were ever foremost in supporting.

At the time this separation took place, the brigade, and we believe all the foreign troops in the French service, were under the command of General Count O'Connell, an uncle to the illustrious Irish Liberator. Thirty-three years previously, while yet very young, Count O'Connell entered the French service as sub-lieutenant in

Clare's regiment of dragoons, and by his intelligence and bravery soon rose to the rank of major-general. At the siege of Gibraltar in 1782, when an unsuccessful attempt was made to prevent Lord Hood from relieving the English garrison, he served on board the admiral's ship, and in command of the French marines performed many acts of daring and prowess, in the course of which he received no less than nine wounds. So marked, indeed, was his conduct during that disastrous engagement, that Louis XVI promoted him to the grade of colonel-commandant, and gave him the charge of the regiment Salm-Salm, a German contingent, full in numbers, but altogether deficient in experience and discipline. O'Connell however had an organizing mind as well as an intrepid spirit, and out of the raw material he was not long in forming one of the best drilled and most orderly regiments in the service. Six years later he was appointed one of the inspectors-general of infantry, and to him that branch of the service is indebted for its present system of organization, which has since been adopted by every country in Europe, and even forms the basis of our own Scott's and Hardee's *Tactics*. In allusion to Count O'Connell's services in his capacity of inspector, Sir Bernard Burke says: —"The French government resolved that the art of war should undergo revision, and a military board was formed for this purpose, comprising four general officers and one colonel. The colonel selected was O'Connell, who was esteemed one of the most scientific officers in the service. Without patronage or family he had risen to a colonelcy before he had attained his fortieth year. Only a few meetings of the board had taken place when the superior officers, struck with the depth and accuracy of information, great military genius, and correct views, displayed by Colonel O'Connell, unanimously agreed to confide to him the revisal of the whole French military code; and he executed the arduous duty so perfectly, that his tactics were those followed in the early campaigns of revolutionized France, adhered to by Napoleon, and adopted by Prussia, Austria, Russia, and England."

Such was the man who, with his foreign legions then in the neighborhood of Paris, prepared to defend the king against the Paris mob, and who doubtless would have strangled the revolution in its cradle if he had been permitted to have done so by that well-meaning but vacillating monarch; and such was the officer who was destined to lead in sorrow and bitterness the last survivors of the historical brigade from the scenes of their former glory. When about to take up their line of march, they halted for a few moments to pay their last respects to their ill-starred sovereign, who was represented on the occasion by his brother. The prince advanced to the front of the brigade, the officers forming a semicircle around him, and spoke as follows:—"We acknowledge, gentlemen, the invaluable services which France, during the lengthened period of one hundred years, has received from the Irish Brigade,—services which we shall never forget, though totally unable to repay. Receive this standard" (it was embroidered with a shamrock and a *fleur-de-lis*), "a pledge of our remembrance, a token of our admiration and respect; and this, generous Hibernians, shall be the motto on your spotless colors—'1692–1792 : *Semper et ubique fidelis.*'"

The principal cause of the departure of the brigade was the hostility daily evinced to foreign soldiers by the incipient revolutionists, and the king was weak enough to yield to their threats in the vain hope of conciliating them. In his imbecility he did not see that the native soldiery had been tampered with, that the loyalty of his foreign levies could be implicitly relied upon, and that, those men out of the way, he was at the mercy, or rather brutality, of the conspirators against his liberty and life. The subsequent career of the once famous brigade was as short it was tragical. Acting on inducements and promises, as specious as they were delusive, the brigade transferred its services to England, hoping, no doubt, to benefit by their presence and conduct, their country and co-religionists at home, and were rewarded by being sent to some of the most pestiferous islands of the West Indies, where the plague and the malaria utterly destroyed the organization in a very few years. Their flag, the last token of royal affection, was deposited in some humble church, we believe, in San Domingo, where we are informed it remains to this day unnoticed and unknown. Count O'Connell, one of the few survivors, returned to Europe, and on the restoration of Louis XVIII, he regained possession of his estates in France, and was restored to his former rank in the army. He died in 1834 at the ripe age of ninety-one years, and with him may be said to have expired the last of the Irish Brigade in the service of France; but so terrible was the dread of that gallant organization to England, that she procured the insertion of a clause in the Treaty of Vienna, in 1815, prohibiting France from ever admitting a brigade of Irishmen in her army.

COUNT O'SHEA.

SWEET REVENGE.

ANOTHER of the survivors of the West India slaughter was O'SHEA who had served with distinction in the brigade on the continent previous to the French Revolution. During the war in St. Domingo he was remarkable for his headlong bravery and invincible determination, but, what with the vicissitudes of battle, and the effects of a tropical climate, he saw his gallant regiment waste away till not a corporal's guard was left to command. He returned home, and applied for a commission in some other battalion, but he was refused even that of an ensign or second lieutenant. The penal laws of that day would not allow such a favor to a Catholic, no matter how great his services, or how matured his experience.

Five long years he spent in inactivity,

endeavoring to obtain a position in the British army, but without avail. At length, his patience becoming exhausted, he resolved to go abroad. "My father," he said to a friend on the eve of his departure, "had nothing to leave me but a sword. That sword I have tendered to the service of my country; she has refused: I have no longer a country. I have offered it to England; I shall now offer it to France. The country that has refused me bread will give me a halter when they get me in their power. The chances of war may put me in their hands: there is my will; do thou be my executor."

The indignant and ill-treated soldier accordingly crossed to France, and was well received by the minister of war, General Clarke, a Franco-Irishman, and by Napoleon, to whom his merits were not unknown, as he had heard of him from Rochambeau, against whom the major had fought in the West Indies. His appointment was a matter of course, and his promotion, even for those stirring times, wonderfully rapid. In six months he had obtained a majority, and in another half-year he found himself in command of a regiment of hussars, having again been promoted on the field for gallant and meritorious conduct. Soon after, he was made governor of Antwerp, where his skill, efficiency, and untiring energy were of infinite service to the country of his adoption. To his ability and exertions was mainly due the failure of what is known as the Walcheren Expedition, disastrous to the arms and prestige of England, as his subsequent conduct, while in command of a corps at the siege of Burgos in Spain, defeated the attempts of the British to capture that city. It is pleasant to know that the halter, to which the English government would have treated him if once in their power, was never brought into requisition, for he was not the sort of person to be easily taken; and the count, for he was created a count of the empire for distinguished services, lived to enjoy a long and honorable old age.

CAPTAIN O'REILLY.

A BRIGADE OFFICER OF THE OLD SCHOOL.

The following amusing sketch of a retired officer of the old brigade, who had returned home to end his days among his friends and kinsfolk, is taken from the "Reminiscences of Michael Kelly." The mixture of many languages, not excepting even his native Gaelic, was by no means unnatural with one who had seen much service in many countries, and who thereby acquired a proficiency in their respective vocabularies.

"Walking on the Parade the second morning of my arrival in Cork," says Mr. Kelly, "Mr. Townsend, of the *Correspondent* newspaper, pointed out a very fine-looking, elderly gentleman standing at the club-house door, and told me that he was one of the most eccentric men in the world. His name was O'Reilly, and he had served many years in the Irish Brigade in Germany and Prussia, where he had been distinguished as an excellent officer. Mr. Townsend added: 'We reckon him here a great epicure, and he piques himself on being a great judge of the culinary art, as well as of wines. His good nature and pleasantry have introduced him to the best society, particularly among the Roman Catholics, where he is always a welcome guest. He speaks French, German, and Italian, and constantly, while speaking English with a determined Irish brogue, mixes all those languages in every sentence. It is immaterial to him whether the person he is talking to understands him or not—on he goes, stop him who can.'

"I was presented to him," continues Mr. Kelly, "and no sooner had the noble captain shaken me by the hand than he exclaimed: '*Bon jour, mon cher Mick! Je suis bien aise de vous voir*, as we say in France. *An bhfhuil tu go maith. J'etois faché* that I missed meeting you when I was last in Dublin; but I was obliged to go to the county Galway to see a brother officer who formerly served with me in Germany—as *herlich ein kerl*, as we say in Germany, as ever smelt gunpowder. *Dair mo laimh—il est brave comme son epée*, as fearless as his sword. Now tell me how go on your brother Joe and brother Mark; your brother Pat, poor fellow, lost his life, I know, in the East Indies—but *c'est la fortune de la guerre*, and he died *avec l'honneur*. Your sister Mary, too—how is she? *Dair a marreann*, by my word she is as good a hearted, kind creature as ever lived; but, *entre nous, soit dit*—she is rather plain, *ma non e bella, quel ch'è bella, e bella quel che piace*, as we say in Italian.'

"Now captain," said Mr. Kelly, "after the flattering encomiums you have bestowed on my sister's beauty, may I ask how you became so well acquainted with my family concerns?"

"'*Parbleu!* my dear Mick,' said the captain, 'well I may be, for sure your mother and my mother were sisters.'

"On comparing notes," adds Kelly, "I

found that such was the fact. When I was a boy, and before I left Dublin for Italy, I remember my mother often mentioning a nephew of hers of the name of O'Reilly, who had been sent to Germany when quite a lad—many years before—to a relative of his father who was in the Irish Brigade at Prague. Young O'Reilly entered the regiment as a cadet, he afterwards went into the Prussian service; but my mother heard no more of him. The captain told me, furthermore, that he had been cheated some years before out of a small property which his father left him in the county Meath, by a man whom he thought his best friend. 'However,' said the captain, 'I had my satisfaction by calling him out and putting a bullet through his hat; but, nevertheless, all the little property that was left me is gone. But, *grace au ciel*, I have never sullied my reputation nor injured mortal, and for that " the gods will take care of Cato." In all my misfortunes, cousin, I have never parted with the family sword, which was never drawn in a dirty cause; and there it hangs now in a little cabin which I have got in the county Meath. Should ever Freddy Jones discard me, I will end my days in *risposo e pace* with the whole universal world.'"

The Frederick Jones mentioned by the captain was proprietor of Crow Street theatre. Jones took such a liking to him the first day he came to dine with him, that O'Reilly became his confidant and deputy-manager for life.

One day, the captain was in the streets of Clonmel when the Tipperary militia was marching out of town. The colonel's father had formerly been a miller and amassed a large fortune, which he bequeathed to the colonel himself. O'Reilly eyed the half-drilled militia and the swaggering but un-soldier-like colonel with the critical scrutiny of a veteran, and then exclaimed: "By the god of war, here comes Marshal *Sacks* and the *flour* of Tipperary at his back!"

DANIEL O'CONNELL.

HIS DUEL WITH D'ESTERRE.

In 1814–15, the future Liberator was fast rising in popular favor, and from his boldness of speech, and legal acumen in evading the tricks and devices of the Castle faction, was already looked upon as the leader of the people and the champion of Catholicity, then prostrated under the infliction of the penal laws. As the tribune of the masses, he was almost as much disliked by the few "loyal," cowardly Catholic noblemen who were still allowed to exist in the country, as he was by the English officials and the Orangemen. Finding it impossible to silence him by persecutions, cajolery, or threats, the latter, twin haters of Ireland, resolved to make away with him at all hazzards, and in a manner more worthy of the dark ages of feudalism than of our supposed advanced century. At that time the Dublin corporation was Orange "to the back bone," and one of its members was a certain J. N. D'Esterre, a man of desperate fortunes, and of great pecuniary embarrassments. He had formerly served as an officer of marines in the British navy, and was remarkable for his cool, reckless daring, and his skill in the use of firearms, particularly the pistol. This was the man therefore selected by the enemies of O'Connell as the instrument of their vengeance, and inducements were held out to him that, if he succeeded in killing the popular leader, honors and emoluments were sure to follow. Goaded to desperation by creditors, and lured by the hope of official distinction, which invariably awaited any attack on the Irish Catholics, individually or collectively, the unfortunate desperado prepared to force a quarrel on O'Connell, and even went so far as to arm himself with a horsewhip and to parade the public streets with the avowed intention of inflicting personal violence on him.

We are not of those who defend the practice of duelling—fortunately, it is fast becoming a thing of the past in all well-ordered communities—but, if any thing could palliate or justify it, such justification can be found in the peculiar circumstances by which O'Connell was then surrounded. The aspiring leader of the most warlike and the bravest people in Europe, he was obliged to demonstrate his courage as well as to display his eloquence and legal lore. While attacked on every side by the mercenary scribes and spouters of the Castle, his refusal to accept a challenge, or his apology for words spoken upon mature deliberation, would have been the signal for falsehoods and slanders that might have cooled the affection and weakened the confidence of the people he was destined to lead out of worse than Egyptian bondage.

As a great deal was said at the time, and probably will continue to be spoken and written about that duel as long as O'Connell's name and fame are discussed, we abridge from the Dublin *Evening Post* and other contemporary and impartial authorities, the particulars of the fatal rencontre, merely premising that in point of skill in the use of his weapon, and experience in such affairs, the Irish champion was far inferior to his antagonist. In point of size, D'Esterre, who was of diminutive stature, had also a decided advantage, while O'Connell, as the event proved, far excelled his opponent in temper, coolness, and that sublime heroism which is only found in those who know they are defending a righteous cause.

On Thursday, the 26th of January, says the *Post*, D'Esterre addressed a letter to O'Connell in the following words:—

"11 *Bachelor's Walk*, *26th January*, 1815.

"Sir: Carrick's paper of the 23d instant (in its report of the debates of a meeting of Catholic gentlemen, on the subject of a petition) states that you have applied the appellation of *beggarly* to the corporation of this city, *calling it a beggarly corporation*—and therefore, as a member of that body, and feeling how painful such is, I beg leave to inquire whether you really used or expressed yourself in any such language? I feel the more justified in calling on you on this occasion, as such language was not warranted or provoked by any thing on the part of the corporation; neither was it consistent with the subject of your debate, or the deportment of the other Catholic gentlemen who were present; and though I view it as so inconsistent in every respect, I am in hopes the editor is under error, and not you. I have further to request your reply in the course of the evening, and remain, sir, your obedient servant,

"J. N. D'ESTERRE.

"*To Counsellor O'Connell, Merrion Square.*"

Mr. O'Connell's answer was as follows:—

"*Merrion Square, January* 27, 1815.

"SIR: In reply to your letter of yesterday, and without either admitting or disclaiming the expression respecting the corporation of Dublin in the print to which you allude, I deem it right to inform you that, from the calumnious manner in which the religion and character of the Catholics of Ireland are treated in that body, no terms attributed to me, however reproachful, can exceed the contemptuous feelings I entertain for that body in its corporate capacity; although doubtless it contains many valuable persons, whose conduct as individuals (I lament) must necessarily be confounded in the acts of a general body. I have only to add that *this letter must close our correspondence on this subject.*

"I am, &c., &c.,

"DANIEL O'CONNELL.

"*To J. N. D'Esterre, Esq.,* 11 *Bachelor's Walk.*"

Mr. D'Esterre was advised to persist in the correspondence, and he addressed another letter (but directed in a different handwriting) to Mr. O'Connell. It was returned to him by Mr. James O'Connell, enclosed in a letter of the following tenor:—

"*Merrion Square, Friday Evening.*

"SIR: From the tenor of your letter of yesterday, my brother did not expect that your next communication would have been made *in writing*. He directed me to open his letters in his absence. Your last letter, bearing a different address from the former one, was opened by me; but upon perceiving the name subscribed, I have declined to read it, and by his directions I return it to you enclosed and *unread*.—I am, sir, your obedient servant,
"JAMES O'CONNELL.
"*To J. N. D'Esterre, Esq., 11 Bachelor's Walk.*"

The preceding letter was penned on Friday, and things remained in this condition until Sunday. On that day Mr. James O'Connell received a note from Mr. D'Esterre, containing disrespectful observations on himself and his brother. Immediately after the receipt of it, James sent his friend, Captain O'Mullane, to Mr. D'Esterre, to say that, when the affair with Daniel was adjusted, he would bring him to account for his conduct to himself peculiarly. Captain O'Mullane at the same time intimated that Counsellor O'Connell was astonished at his not hearing in what he conceived *the proper way* from Mr. D'Esterre. Nothing further happened on Sunday, and on Monday morning, Mr. Lidwill—who remained several days, to be the friend of Mr. O'Connell—left town for home, despairing of any issue being put to the controversy; besides which, some members of Mr. Lidwill's family were seriously indisposed.

Monday passed, and on Tuesday considerable sensation was created by a rumor that Mr. D'Esterre was advised to go to the Four Courts to offer Mr. O'Connell personal violence. Neither of the parties came in contact, but it seems that Mr. D'Esterre was met on one of the quays by Mr Richard O'Gorman, who remonstrated with him to this effect: " You conceive," said he, "that you received an offence from Mr. O'Connell; if so, your course is to demand satisfaction. This, I understand, you have not as yet done, but if you are now resolved to do it, I undertake, on forfeiture of having a riddle made of my body, to have Mr. O'Connell on the ground in half an hour." This occurred about three o'clock, but no challenge followed. About four, it was understood that Mr. D'Esterre was on the streets, and Mr. O'Connell traversed the city with one or two friends, but did not come across his antagonist. A multitude soon collected about O'Connell, who used several expedients to avoid them. He went into Tuthill's in Dawson Street at one time, and came out through the stable-yard. Still, however, a crowd pressed on, among whom there could not be less than five hundred gentlemen, all of whom seemed carried away with a singular enthusiasm in favor of "the man of the people." Mr. O'Connell then had no other resource left but to take refuge in a house in Exchequer Street. In a short time, however, he was assailed by the most formidable interruption he had yet encountered. Judge Day entered in his magisterial capacity to put him under arrest. The Honorable Justice said he would be satisfied if he had the guarantee of Mr. O'Connell's honor that he would proceed no further in the business. " It is not my duty as a duellist," said O'Connell, " to be the aggressor; I therefore pledge my honor that I shall not be the aggressor—further, however, I must tell you, no human consideration will induce me to go."

In the meantime, it was observed that Mr. D'Esterre was in a shop in Grafton Street, surrounded by a number of friends. We have heard that Mr. James O'Connell noticed on the countenance of one of them a leer, which provoked him to use an insulting expression. Nothing, however, in the way of a demand of explanation followed. Tuesday then ended without a challenge. Some of Mr. O'Connell's friends went to the play in the evening, and they brought many persons to account for expressions unfavorable to Mr. O'Connell, which they conceived they overheard. There was a clergyman questioned, who defended himself by mentioning his profession; as to the others, they all, *uná voce*, declared they meant nothing offensive to Mr. O'Connell. No challenge of any kind then grew out of Tuesday's proceedings. On Wednesday morning, however, it was at length intimated to Mr. O'Connell that Mr. D'Esterre intended to call upon him for a meeting.

At nine o'clock on that day, Sir E. Stanley was knocking at O'Connell's door, and he was introduced to the lawyer in his study. Sir Edward opened his commission by saying that he wished to get an explanation from O'Connell relative to D'Esterre's affair. "Sir, I will hold no conversation with you on that subject," replied O'Connell; "my friend is Major MacNamara—here is his address" (giving it to Sir Edward). "You must apply to him for whatever information you desire." "Oh! but, sir," said the civic knight, who was nervously anxious to glide out of the difficulty in which he found his faction involved, if he could do so without subversion of character, "I only wish to say a few words in explanation." O'Connell waved his hand and persisted in refusing to listen to the representations of Sir Edward, and the knight slowly took his departure with a rueful visage, apparently much dejected by the failure of his embassy. Twelve o'clock was fixed upon for the nomination of hour and place. There was some overture made to enlarge the time, but Mr. O'Connell's friend would not consent. We should mention that this friend was Major MacNamara of Doolen, in the county Clare, a Protestant gentleman attached to no party, and of the highest respectability. He is the descendant of some of the most distinguished of our Irish chieftains. Of the extent of his property we need not give a better description than that he is able to poll six hundred freeholders. The friend of Mr. D'Esterre was Sir Edward Stanley.

At twelve o'clock on Wednesday, the day appointed, Sir Edward called on Major

MacNamara at the lodgings of the latter, when the knight began by lamenting the necessity which forced him to make this application to Major MacNamara on behalf of his friend, D'Esterre, adding that he hoped the matter might yet be adjusted by an amicable explanation. "If you expect an apology or explanation from O'Connell, you must be disappointed," said Major MacNamara. "He has given no offence to D'Esterre,—he has done him no injury; therefore I must tell you it will be a waste of words and loss of time to speak further on a topic which has already, and for so long a time, engaged the public attention."

"Then, sir, it is my duty to deliver you a message from Mr. D'Esterre to Mr. O'Connell," said Sir Edward.

"Very well," rejoined Major Mac-Namara; "it is my privilege to appoint a time and place, and I fix on this afternoon at three o'clock for the meeting, and Bishop's Court in the county Kildare as the place."

The promptitude of this arrangement seemed to disconcert Sir Edward, whose visage became singularly discomposed. He faltered out a request to Major MacNamara to postpone it to two o'clock the following day, or until an early hour the succeeding morning, or even till half-past four that afternoon; but MacNamara would on no account consent to postpone the meeting further than half-past three on the day on which they were speaking. These points being adjusted, Major MacNamara observed that, as the duellists had no personal quarrel, nor any rancorous feeling of private animosity, he supposed all parties would be satisfied when each gentleman discharged one pistol. The moderation of this suggestion stimulated Sir Edward to swagger a little. "No, sir," he replied in a hectoring tone, 'that will not do; if they fired five-and-twenty shots each, Mr. D'Esterre will never leave the ground until Mr. O'Connell makes an apology."

"Well, then, if blood be your object, blood you shall have, by G——!" replied Major MacNamara.

A slight shower of snow was whitening

the ground as O'Connell and his friends rolled through James's Street on their way to Bishop's Court. This place is about twelve miles from the city, and constitutes a portion of Lord Ponsonby's demesne. The hour appointed was half-past three o'clock. At three precisely—we can speak confidently, for we now speak from personal knowledge—Mr. O'Connell, attended by his second, and Surgeon Macklin, and a number of friends, was on the ground. About four, Mr. D'Esterre, attended only by Surgeon Peele, Sir Edward Stanley, his second, Mr. Piers, and a Mr. D'Esterre of Limerick, appeared. There was some conversation between the seconds as to position, mode of fire, &c., which, added to other sources of delay, occupied forty minutes.

Meantime a considerable number of strangers came dropping in, one by one, to the scene of the altercation, and formed a large concourse of silent, watchful, and attentive spectators. Seeing this, Sir Edward, again addressing Major Mac-

Namara, expressed an apprehension (which he affected to entertain) as to the safety of himself and D'Esterre in case O'Connell should fall. He added, that it was his firm conviction, should his friend fight in that place on that day, the life of D'Esterre's friends must be jeopardized.

"This affair has been long the subject of public conversation," answered Connell O'Connell, a relative of the Agitator, "and your friend has been the aggressor: if you now quit the ground without fighting, I must consider you as cowards and ruffians; and as to you, Sir Edward, I shall call on you personally to make reparation for an additional insult."

On hearing this last remark, Sir Edward's indecision vanished. He proceeded at once to prepare his pistols, and to place D'Esterre in the position and on the ground of a duellist. Major MacNamara—in person one of the finest men in Europe—then advanced and said that the choice of the ground must be determined by an appeal to chance; they should throw up a coin, and whoever guessed while the money was in the air the side which should turn up, should enjoy the privilege of choosing his ground. This arrangement was agreed to by Sir Edward. A piece of money went whirling into the air, one party cried, and Major MacNamara proved the winner. During this interval, Mr. D'Esterre took occasion to say, that his quarrel with Mr. O'Connell was not of a religious nature; he had no animosity whatsoever to the Catholics or their leaders. At forty minutes past four o'clock the combatants were on the ground. They both displayed the greatest coolness and courage. As to Mr. O'Connell, we never saw him in better spirits or more composed; indeed his cheerfulness was the astonishment of every spectator.

It would be injustice to Mr. D'Esterre, whatever opinion we may have of the part he espoused, or rather the party who stimulated him to this act, to deny that he appeared perfectly self-possessed. We understand, when it had been agreed by the seconds that the opponents were to take their ground with a case of pistols each, to use as they might think proper, Sir E. Stanley, Mr. D'Esterre's friend, addressed Major MacNamara, Mr. O'Connell's friend, as follows:

"Well, sir, when each has discharged his case of pistols, I hope the affair will be considered as terminated, and that we leave the ground."

Major MacNamara:—"Sir, you may, of course, take your friend from the ground when you please. You, sir, are the challenger, and you may retire from the ground whenever you think proper; but I shall not enter into any such condition as you propose. However, it is probable that there may be no occasion to discharge the whole of a case of pistols."

The friends of both parties retired, and the combatants, having a pistol in each hand, with directions to discharge them at their discretion, prepared to fire. They levelled, and before the lapse of a second both shots were heard. Mr. D'Esterre was first, and missed. His bullet struck the ground.

The moment D'Esterre discharged his pistol, he bent his right knee and wheeled away a little, as if he sought to avoid the sight of O'Connell, or wished to present his back to his antagonist; but why he did so— whether from contempt, levity, or apprehension—it is impossible to say. Mr. O'Connell's shot followed instantaneously, and took effect in the groin of his antagonist, about an inch below the hip. Mr. D'Esterre of course fell, and both the surgeons hastened to him. They found the ball had traversed the hip, passed through the bladder, and possibly touched the spine. It could not be found. There was an immense effusion of blood. All parties prepared to move towards home, and arrived in town before eight o'clock. We were extremely glad to perceive that Major MacNamara and many respectable gentlemen assisted in procuring the best accommodation for the wounded man. They sympathized in his sufferings, and expressed themselves to Sir Edward Stanley as extremely well pleased that a transaction, which they considered most uncalled-for, had not terminated in the death of D'Esterre. We need not describe the emotions which burst forth along the road and through the town when it was ascertained that Mr. O'Connell was safe.

Another authority says: "Nothing could be more correct or honorable than the conduct of the parties upon the ground. Mr. O'Connell displayed all the gentleness of heart so peculiarly belonging to his character, and his particular request to his medical friend, before taking his ground, was this: 'Should any fatality happen to my opponent, I entreat you to consider him as your patient—treat him with all the care you would devote to me.'"

Mr. Fagan says, in his account of the affair:—"It was reported in Dublin that Mr. O'Connell was shot; and a party of dragoons were despatched from Dublin for the protection of Mr. D'Esterre. On their way the officer by whom they were commanded met, on its return, the carriage containing Mr. O'Connell and his brother. The officer called on the postilions to stop, whereupon Mr. James O'Connell pulled down the window. The officer, addressing him, asked if they had been present at the duel, to which he replied in the affirmative. The officer then said, 'Is it true Mr. O'Connell has been shot?' Mr. James O'Connell replied, 'No—the reverse is the fact; Mr. D'Esterre has unfortunately fallen.' The announcement had a visible effect upon the military; they were not prepared for the intelligence, and something like consternation was exhibited. The carriage was allowed to proceed—the military party being evidently not aware who were its occupants.

"When D'Esterre fell, the spectators on the field could not refrain from giving expression to their feelings—they actually shouted; and a young collegian who was present, and who is now an excellent exemplary Protestant clergyman, was so carried away by the general feeling as to fling up his hat in the air, and shout, 'Huzza for O'Connell!' Very different was the conduct of the three occupants of O'Connell's carriage. They displayed no exultation. The moment D'Esterre fell they went off; and though the place of meeting was near Naas, they were close to Dublin before a single word was exchanged between them. At last O'Connell broke the silence, saying: 'I fear he is dead, he fell so suddenly. Where do you think he was hit?' 'In the head, I think,' said his medical friend. 'That cannot be—I aimed low; the ball must have entered near the thigh.' This will be considered a remarkable observation, when it is recollected where, as was subsequently found, the wound was inflicted. It shows the perfect coolness and humanity of O'Connell. Being one of the surest shots that ever fired a pistol, he could have hit his antagonist where he pleased. But his object was merely, in self-defence, to wound him in no mortal part; and he aimed low with that intention."

"His contest with O'Connell," says the late Mark O'Callaghan, "has rescued D'Esterre's name from that miserable obscurity which is the general fate of most human beings. D'Esterre was a brave man gone astray. Were Ireland a nation, like those once despicable countries which raised themselves to that state, such as the United Provinces of Holland, or the United States of America,—had Ireland a navy like them, had D'Esterre commanded a ship with a crew of Irish lads in that navy, we would place him alongside a ship of any other nation, far or near, and lay two to one he would soon make her strike her flag. But such was not his fate. He served with thousands of forgotten Irishmen as an officer in the English navy."

O'Connell's victory—for the duel had become an event of national importance—created the greatest excitement in the capital and throughout the country, and was the occasion of general popular rejoicing by the nationalists, and corresponding chagrin to the Orangemen and British factions. From the archbishop of Dublin to the humblest peasant, the escape of the future Emancipator was a subject of congratulation, and bonfires blazed on a thousand hills, in the yet unregenerated land.

D'Esterre's wound proved to be mortal, and he died two days after the fatal shot, regretted by none more sincerely than his antagonist and his friends. O'Connell's munificent offer to provide for his widow and her children was declined, but he afterwards had the satisfaction of assisting one of D'Esterre's daughters when in indigent circumstances, and of settling upon her a handsome annuity. There was no prosecution; and so an event, which, if it had ended otherwise, might have been fatal to the hopes of the Irish Catholics, of that generation at least, passed into history.

FLOOD AND FIELD.

A SAILOR ON SHORE.

THERE is not, perhaps, in the annals of shipwreck, a personal narrative more deeply distressing, or more painfully interesting, than that of Captain Riley. Were there not the most ample testimony to his excellent moral character and unimpeachable veracity, we might be led to withhold our belief from some parts of his narrative, on the simple ground that human nature, on the one hand, was utterly incapable of inflicting, and, on the other, of enduring, such hardships and sufferings as this gentleman and his poor shipwrecked companions had to undergo,—sufferings which, as Captain Riley truly says, "have been as great and as various as ever fell to the lot of humanity."

The brig "Commerce," commanded by Captain Riley, with a crew of ten persons, was wrecked on the coast of Africa, on the 28th of August, 1815. With some difficulty the crew, many of whom were Americans, reached the shore, and secured a small quantity of provisions, and tools to repair their boat, in which they hoped to reach the Cape de Verde Islands. All hopes of this were, however, soon rendered abortive by the appearance of a party of Arabs, who burnt their trunks and chests, carried off their provisions, and stove in the wine and water-casks. The crew escaped to their boat, but Mr. Riley was left behind. One of the Arabs seized hold of him by the throat, and with a scimitar at his breast, gave him to understand there was money on board, and it must instantly be brought ashore.

When the ship was wrecked, Mr. Riley had divided the dollars among the crew. On being informed of the demands of the Arabs, he hailed the men, and told them what the savages required; a bucket was accordingly sent on shore with about a thousand dollars. An old Arab instantly laid hold of it, and forcing Riley to accompany him, they all went behind the sand hills to divide the spoil. In this situation he felt himself very uneasy, and, in order to regain the beach, he made signs that there was still more money remaining in the ship. The hint succeeded; and under the idea of getting it, they allowed him again to hail his people, when, instead of money, he desired them to send on shore Antonio Michael (an old man they had taken in at New Orleans), as the only possible means left for him of effecting his own escape. The Arabs finding, on his reaching the shore, that he had brought no money with him, struck him, pricked him with their sharp knives, and stripped him of all his clothes. Mr. Riley seized this opportunity of springing from his keepers, and plunged into the sea. On rising through the surf, he perceived the old Arab within ten feet of him, up to his chin in water, with his spear ready to strike him; but another surf rolling at that instant over him, saved his life, and he reached the lee of the wreck in safety. The remorseless brutes wreaked their vengeance on poor Antonio, by plunging a spear into his body, which laid him lifeless at their feet.

The wreck was, by this time, going rapidly to pieces: the long boat writhed like an old basket. The crew had neither provisions nor water; neither oars nor a rudder to the boat; neither compass nor quadrant to direct their course; yet, hopeless as their situation was, and expecting to be swallowed up by the first surf, they resolved to try their fate on the ocean, rather than to encounter death from the relentless savages on shore. By great exertion they succeeded in finding a water-cask, out of which they filled four gallons into a keg. One of the seamen, Porter, stole on shore by the hawser, and brought on board two oars, with a small bag of money which they had buried, containing about four hundred dollars. They also contrived to get together a few pieces of salt pork, a live pig weighing about twenty pounds, about four pounds of figs, a spar for the boat's mast, a jib, and a mainsail. Every thing being ready, the crew said their prayers; and the wind ceasing to blow, the boat was launched through the breakers. In this miserable boat they determined to stand out into the wide ocean. After being six days at sea, it was driven on the rocks, and completely stove, but the crew again reached the shore.

On the next morning they set out from the place where they had been cast, which, as it afterwards appeared, was Cape Barbas, not far from Cape Blanco. They proceeded easterly close to the water's edge, for three days, when they encountered a large company of Arabs who were watering their camels. The shipwrecked mariners bowed themselves to the ground with every mark of submission, and by signs implored their compassion, but in vain. The whole party were in an instant stripped naked to the skin, and the Arabs began to fight most furiously for the booty, and especially for getting possession of the prisoners. "Six or eight of them," says Captain Riley, whose narrative we now quote, "were about me, one hauling me one way, and one another. The one who stript us, stuck to us as his lawful property, signifying, 'You may have the others, these are mine.'

"They cut at each other over my head, and on every side of me, with their bright weapons, which fairly whizzed through the air within an inch of my naked body and on every side of me, now hacking each other's arms apparently to the bone; men laying their ribs bare with gashes, while their heads, hands, and thighs received a full share of cuts and wounds. The blood streaming from every gash, ran down their bodies, coloring and heightening the natural hideousness of their appearance. I had expected to be cut to pieces in this dreadful affray, but was not injured.

"The battle over, I saw my distressed companions divided among the Arabs, and all going towards the drove of camels, though they were at some distance from me. We too were delivered into the hands of two old women, who urged us on with sticks towards the camels. Naked and barefooted, we could not go very fast, and I showed the women my mouth, which was parched white as frost, and without a sign of moisture. When we got near the well, one of the women called for another, who came to us with a wooden bowl, that held, I should guess, about a gallon of water, and setting it on the ground, made myself and Dick kneel down and put our heads into it like camels. I drank, I suppose, half a gallon, though I had been very particular in cautioning the men against drinking too much at a time, in case they ever came to water. I now experienced how much easier it was to preach, than to practise aright. They then led us to the well, the water of which was nearly as black and disgusting as stale bilgewater. A large bowl was now filled with it, and a little sour camel's-milk poured from a goatskin into it; this tasted to me delicious, and we all drank of it till our stomachs were literally filled. We now begged for something to eat, but these Arabs had nothing for themselves, and seemed very sorry it was not in their power to give us some food. There were at and about the well, I should think, about one hundred persons, men, women, and children, and from four to five hundred camels, large and small. The sun beat fiercely upon us, and our skins seemed actually to fry like meat before the fire. These people continued to draw water for their camels, of which the animals drank enormous quantities."

The party travelled southeast over a plain covered with small sharp stones, which lacerated their feet dreadfully. About midnight they halted, and for the first time got about a pint of pure camel's-milk each. The wind was chilling cold; they lay on the sharp stones, perfectly naked; their bodies blistered and mangled, and the stones piercing their naked flesh to the ribs. On the morning of the 11th (September), a pint of milk was divided among four of them, and they got nothing more until midnight, when they were allowed a little milk and water. They continued travelling in the desert, enduring all the miseries of hunger, thirst, and fatigue, with every addition Arab cruelty could inflict, until they reached Wadnoon. Sidi Hamet, an African trader, who had purchased them of the old Arab, however, became the means of their deliverance. He told Mr. Riley, that he must write a letter to his friend at Suara, desiring him to pay the money for the ransom of himself and people, when they should be free. A scrap of paper, a reed, and some black liquor, were then brought to Mr. Riley, who briefly wrote the circumstances of the loss of the ship, his captivity, &c., adding: "Worn down to the bone by the most dreadful of all sufferings, naked, and a slave, I implore your pity, and trust that such distress will not be suffered to plead in vain." The letter was addressed, "To the English, French, Spanish, or American Consuls, or any Christian merchants in Mogadore." The anxiety of the captives may be well imagined. For seven days after Hamet's departure, they were shut up in a yard during the day, where cows, sheep, and asses rested; and locked up all night in a dreary cellar.

On the evening of the eighth day, a Moor came into the enclosure, and brought a letter from Mr. Wiltshire, the English consul, stating, that he had agreed to the demands of Sidi Hamet, whom he kept as a hostage for their safe appearance, and that the bearer would conduct them to Mogadore. He had also sent them clothes and provisions; and thus accoutred and fortified, they set out under their new conductor, who brought them safe to Mogadore, where they were most kindly received by Mr. Wiltshire.

We need only add that the brave Irish sailor, whose average weight was usually about two hundred pounds, was found upon being put into the scales to have lost over half that weight during his captivity.

THE 88th RANGERS.

CONNAUGHT ROBBERS.

The following anecdote is told of the conduct of two Irish regiments under Wellington at the battle of Fuentes d'Onoro, one of the most critical of that general's many engagements on the Peninsula. The force of the sarcasm uttered by one of the 88th, lies in the fact, that General Picton was in the habit of using the term half in condemnation and half in good humor.

"Fourteenth! Fourteenth!" cried a voice from behind, and at the same moment a staff officer, without his hat, and his horse bleeding from a recent sabre-cut, came up. "You must move to the rear, Colonel Merivale; the French have gained the heights. Move round by the causeway—bring up your squadrons as quickly as you can, and support the infantry."

In a moment we were in our saddles. But scarcely was the word to "fall in" given, when a loud cheer rent the very air; the musketry seemed suddenly to cease, and the mass which seemed to struggle up the heights wavered, broke, and turned.

"What can that be?" said Merivale. "What can it mean?"

"I can tell you, sir," said I, proudly, while I felt my heart as though it would bound from my bosom.

"And what is it, boy? Speak!"

"There it goes again! That was an Irish shout,—the 88th are at them!"

"By Jove! here they come," said Hampden: "God help the Frenchmen now!"

The words were not well spoken, when the coats of our gallant fellows were seen dashing through the vineyard.

"The steel, boys—nothing but the steel!" shouted a loud voice from the crag above our heads.

I looked up. It was the stern Picton himself who spoke.

"The 88th now led the pursuit, and

sprang from rock to rock in all the mad impetuosity of battle; and like some mighty billow rolling before the gale, the French went down the heights.

"Gallant 88th! Gloriously done!" cried Picton as he waved his hat.

"Ar'n't we Connaught robbers, now?" shouted a rich brogue, as its owner, breathless and bleeding, pressed forward in the charge.

A hearty burst of laughter mingled with the din of the battle.

"Now for it, boys! Now for *our* work," said Merivale, drawing his sabre as he spoke. "Forward and charge!"

We waited not a second bidding, but, bursting from our concealment, galloped down on the broken column. It was no regular charge, but an indiscriminate rush. Scarcely offering resistance, the enemy fell beneath our sabres, or the still more deadly bayonets of the infantry, who were inextricably mingled up in the conflict.

The chase was followed up for above

half a mile, when we fell back, fortunately, in good time; for the French had opened a heavy fire from their artillery, and, regardless of their own retreating column, poured a shower of grape among our squadrons. As we retired, the straggling files of the Rangers joined us,—their faces and accoutrements blackened and begrimed with powder; many of them, themselves wounded, had captured prisoners: and one huge fellow of the grenadier company was seen driving before him a no less powerful Frenchman, and to whom, as he turned from time to time reluctantly and scowled upon his jailor, the other vociferated some Irish imprecation, whose harsh intentions were made most palpably evident by a flourish of a drawn bayonet.

GENERAL THOMAS W. SWEENY.

BATTLES OF CERRO GORDO AND SHILOH.

When the Mexican war with this country broke out in 1846, it evoked a military spirit in all classes of the community, which had slumbered for more than a quarter of a century. The farmer left his plow in the furrow, and the mechanic dropped the tools of his trade; the lawyer threw aside his books, and the merchant abandoned his counting-house, all eager to take up arms and sustain the dignity of the American flag. Amongst the first and most eager to volunteer from this city was a young printer, then in the first flush of manhood, named Thomas W. Sweeny, who, abandoning home and friends, entered hopefully on the perilous path which leads to military fame, but more often to the grave.

As a member of the Tompkins Blues, an independent militia company, he had already enjoyed the semblance of military life; but he was now desirous to witness its stern realities. When the captain and some members of that company volunteered for the war as part of the 1st New York Volunteers, he went with it as second lieutenant; and, on his arrival in Mexico, had the double pleasure of being elected first lieutenant, and of having his regiment assigned to the brigade of his countryman, General James Shields, then forming part of Scott's command.

Up to and including the battle of Cerro Gordo, Lieutenant Sweeny was ever at his post, and when any fighting was to be done, he was always to be found prepared to take his share of it.

We next find him at Cherubusco, with his right arm badly wounded, cheering on his men, where, notwithstanding the pain of his shattered limb, he continued in action till victory crowned the American arms. This persistence in remaining on the field so long nearly cost him his life, on account of the intense heat of the weather, and the difficulty afterwards of obtaining medical assistance; as it was, he lost his right arm, which suffered amputation, and was thus prevented taking any further part in the war during the continuation of hostilities.

On the restoration of peace, Lieutenant Sweeny returned to New York, where he was the recipient of very flattering attentions from the citizens of all classes, as well as those of Brooklyn, and particularly from his fellow-craftsmen, who felt proud that one of their number should have so distinguished himself. The Government of the United States, also, in appreciation of his gallant services, commissioned him as second lieutenant in the 2d U. S. Infantry—a compliment more rare and valuable at that time than it has since become—and sent him to the Pacific coast, near the scene of his former dangers and triumphs. It was while in the far West that he was assigned to the charge of Fort Yuma, a stockaded log-house, which, with only ten men, he held for as many months, surrounded by hostile Indians bent on its capture, and entirely cut off from succor or communication with the white settlements.

In 1851, he was promoted to be first lieutenant; in January 1861, a captain; and, in October, 1863, he rose to the rank of major in the regular service. In 1854 he returned to New York, and was ordered on regimental recruiting service; and in the spring of the following year was ordered to Nebraska, where he served with his regiment during the Sioux war.

Meanwhile the Civil War broke out, and Captain Sweeny was assigned to the command of the arsenal at St. Louis, a post of great importance at that time, as a heavy force of the rebels had assembled in the neighborhood under General Frost, with the design of capturing the large stores of guns and ammunition contained in the arsenal, seizing St. Louis, and drawing the State out of the Union. On the surrender of those malcontents at Camp Jackson, Sweeny, who was second in command of the Union troops, conducted the negotiations which led to their discomfiture and surrender.

He was appointed brigadier-general in the three months' service, and served with General Lyon in the Missouri campaign, which terminated with the battle of Wilson's Creek, where Lyon was killed; but, though the victory was decidedly in favor of the Union troops, the officer who next took command ordered a retreat. This General Sweeny strenuously opposed, urging that that was the time to show firmness and strike a decisive blow, and offering to lead his brigade alone against the discomfited and disheartened enemy; but his remonstrance was unheeded, and a retreat was commenced which proved more disastrous to our troops than the loss of a battle, while the effect it had on the spirit of the nation, at that stage of the war, was most lamentable and depressing. On this battle-field he got a wound in the leg.

In October, of the same year, he accompanied General Fremont's army into South-

Western Missouri as adjutant-general of the 5th Division, commanded by General McKinstry.

In January, 1862, he was appointed colonel of the 52d Illinois Volunteers, and ordered to report to General Grant, who was then besieging Fort Donelson. At the battle of Shiloh he commanded a brigade of six regiments, and received no less than three wounds, one of which came near depriving him of his left arm, and had two horses killed under him. He was wounded again at the battle of Corinth (3d and 4th October, 1862), where he had another horse killed under him.

In November, 1862, he was appointed brigadier-general of volunteers, and was ordered to North Alabama to attack General Roddy, who was greatly annoying the Federals, and succeeded in driving him out of Tuscumbia. In February, 1863, he commanded the right wing of the column sent into Northern Alabama to cover Colonel Streight's movement on Rome, but, from some unaccountable delay on the part of the latter, Forrest prevented him from accomplishing the object of the expedition.

Yet, notwithstanding his maimed condition and his numerous wounds, General Sweeny was able to take an active part in the war till its final close. He commanded a division under Lieutenant-General Sherman in his celebrated march to the sea, and, we have reason to believe, enjoyed the esteem and confidence of that distinguished soldier in a very high degree. The general is now in his fifty-first year (having been born in Cork in 1822), forty-one of which have been spent in this country, and, though many times wounded, seems as eager for a fight as when he first embarked on a career in which he has earned so much honorable distinction.

He is now on the Retired List of the army. The following is the order under which he was retired:—

"HEAD-QUARTERS OF THE UNITED STATES,
"ADJUTANT-GENERAL'S OFFICE,
"WASHINGTON, May 11, 1870.

"1. A Board of Examination having found Major

Thomas W. Sweeny, U. S. Army, unassigned, 'incapacitated for active service, and that said incapacity is due primarily to a wound received in the battle of Churubusco, Mexico, while a second lieutenant of the First New York Volunteer Infantry, on the 20th of August, 1847, which occasioned the amputation of his right arm at the middle third; and, secondly, to a gunshot wound received in the right leg at the battle of Wilson Creek, Missouri, August 10, 1861, while acting as Inspector-General to Brigadier-General Lyon, and at which time he, Major Sweeny, was a Brigadier-General of the three months' volunteers, under an election of the officers approved by Brigadier-General Lyon; and, thirdly, by a gunshot wound in the flesh of the left arm above the elbow, received at the battle of Shiloh, Tennessee, while commanding a brigade; these several wounds being aggravated by long and faithful service and exposure in the line of duty,' the President directs that his name be placed upon the list of retired officers of that class in which the disability results from long and faithful service, or from wounds or injury in the line of duty. In accordance with section 32 of the act approved July 28, 1866, Major Sweeny is, by direction of the President, retired with the full rank of Brigadier-General.

* * * * * *

"By command of General SHERMAN.

"E. D. TOWNSEND, Adjutant-General.

"J. R. MARTIN, Assistant Adjutant-General"

GENERAL MICHAEL CORCORAN.

THE 69TH AT BULL RUN.

MICHAEL CORCORAN had arrived at manhood before he left his native country to seek a home in America, and, selecting New York as his future residence, early set about identifying himself with the interests of its citizens, and preparing to qualify himself for the performance of the duties imposed upon him by virtue of his naturalization. As soon as it was possible, he joined the 69th militia as a line officer, and was successively promoted to major, lieutenant-colonel, and colonel.

He was acting in this latter capacity when the Prince of Wales visited this country in 1860, and upon his regiment being ordered out by the major-general commanding the division, he refused to obey; and, taking upon himself the sole responsibility, prohibited the promulgation of the order by his subordinate officers. Naturally, he did not feel inclined to see an Irish-American organization used to swell an ovation offered to the eldest son of Queen Victoria and the future king of England, who appeared among us as the representative of a power which has always endeavored to crush liberty and independence in the land of his birth, and to drive millions of his countrymen into poverty and exile. Technically, we think, he was also right, for we doubt very much if the officers commanding divisions or brigades in our State militia have any authority to call upon their commands, peremptorily, for any such purpose as a civic pageant. However, for this supposed breach of military discipline, he was put under the form of arrest, a court-martial was appointed to try him, and had actually commenced its sessions when the civil war broke out and Fort Sumter was bombarded and taken.

Then the militia of this and the other

States were called into service, and the 69th, being one of the first to volunteer, through its lieutenant-colonel, Robert Nugent, the court-martial was dissolved, the charges dropped, and the colonel, amid the warm congratulations of his friends, again assumed command.

On the 23d of April, the 69th left New York for the defence of the national capital. It was composed of nearly every officer of the organization and about two hundred regular members: the shortness of the time allowed, and the peculiar circumstances of many of the rank and file, precluded the possibility of their accompanying their comrades at that time. This deficiency, however, was more than amply supplied by the numbers of recruits who offered themselves during the two previous days and up to the very moment the regiment took up its line of march. It is no exaggeration to say that, during the interval between the receipt of the President's requisition and the departure of the 69th, at least three thousand stalwart Irish adopted citizens presented themselves for enrolment; but, as only a limited number could be accepted, the majority were obliged to go away disappointed, to find an outlet for their patriotic zeal in some other regiment. We have ourselves seen, on the 23d of April, in Prince Street, where the headquarters were, and in Bond Street, where the line was formed, hundreds of fine-looking men, actually praying with tears in their eyes to be allowed to join the ranks. As it was, the majority of those accepted could only be furnished with arms and blankets, and in this condition, the latter rolled up and slung scarf-wise, they left New York, as pugnacious and enthusiastic a body of men as were ever hurled against an enemy.

A short stay on the Annapolis and Washington Railroad and a brief sojourn at Georgetown preceded their entry into Virginia, where for a couple of months they were engaged in building Fort Corcoran, on the south side of the Potomac, commanding the approach to the capital *via* the Aqueduct Bridge, and in drilling and practising the simple manœuvres most likely to be brought into requisition in case of actual conflict. Colonel Corcoran on this occasion paid the strictest attention to his men, not only in teaching them the rudiments of tactics and the manual of arms, but in seeing them supplied with proper uniforms, muskets, equipments, and ammunition. He was well versed in the theory of his new calling, and was an unbending disciplinarian; but withal, a kind and ever-indulgent commandant. In the latter part of May he was joined by Captain Thomas Meagher, with a company of zouaves, all picked men, young, intelligent, and eager for battle; and this, constituting the tenth company of the regiment, raised its strength to nearly thirteen hundred effectives.

At length the desired order for a general advance was issued. Patterson, it was expected, would be able to hold Johnson and his rebels in the Shenandoah Valley, while McDowell and his troops were to attack Beauregard and his force, then in position at Manassas. The 69th, forming a portion of Sherman's brigade and Tyler's division, left their quarters on the 16th of July, and advanced, with the other portions of the Union army, by easy marches to Centreville. Here a halt took place for a couple of days, and, a council of war being held, it was resolved to attack the enemy in three columns,—one at Blackburn's Ford on the left, one at the Stone Bridge in the centre, and the other some distance up Bull Run on the extreme right. The 69th formed part of this latter column.

The 23d of July was selected for the engagement, and early on the morning of that day McDowell's army was in motion; but, though the plans were well conceived, their defective execution was apparent from the very first movement, and ended in utter defeat. In fact, on both sides, a succession of the greatest blunders was observable, which can only be attributed to the inefficiency and want of experience of the general officers. It is now well known, from the reports published by the generals on either side, that both armies were running away at the same time, and that it was only the fortuitous arrival of the rebel General Johnson on the field that saved Beauregard's troops from being completely routed. On our side, the column that had the shortest distance to go was moved first, and, getting prematurely into action, found the others out of supporting distance. Thus Bull Run battle may be said to have been fought piecemeal, and to have been lost in detail.

When the 69th crossed, late in the morning, they formed a long and splendid line, and advanced quickly and in good order on the enemy's left. As soon as they came within range they were saluted with a heavy artillery fire and a discharge of musketry, which brought down several of their men, killing the major, the heroic Haggerty, and dismounting Capt. Meagher by disabling his horse. One wild cheer that rang over the plain of Manassas, and a steady fire of musketry, answered this challenge, and many a man went down, and stout hearts quailed, before that gallant front. "Still on they marched and fired."

Twice did the enemy essay to stop their progress, and were as often repulsed: in vain did they ply their grape, spherical-case, and shrapnel: the irrepressible Irishmen would not be stayed. Their orders were to beat the enemy, and they were resolved to do it; and had some other regiments evinced the like determination on that day, the contest would soon have been ended and the rebellion probably crushed in the bud.

It has been asserted that the men of the 69th fought naked from the waist upward, but this is a pure invention. The day was exceedingly sultry, and many divested themselves of their knapsacks, haversacks, and superfluous clothing, so that they could go into the fight untrammelled—for Irishmen, when they go into action, like to be unencumbered—and this circumstance, we presume, gave rise to the story of their nudity. The fabrication, it may be remarked, also obtained additional currency from those who wished to attach an odor of savageness to their bravery, though it is well known to all who have any knowledge of our late civil war, that a more considerate, humane, and even chivalrous spirit could not have been exhibited by the troops of any nation towards their opponents, than that which peculiarly distinguished the Irish in the United States' service.

In the impetuous and irresistible attack on the enemy's position, Colonel Corcoran was ever in advance of his men, cheering them by his words and animating them by his example; and it was only when the rout became general, and his line was without support, that, with a heavy heart, he gave the order to retreat. This was done in tolerably good order; the Run was recrossed, and as the rebels pressed close upon them, they formed a square to resist their attack and cover the retreat. It was, however, useless. In the confusion that ensued, the mass of fugitives, two-thirds of the entire army, surrounded and swept away the 69th, which became so inextricably mixed up with them that the colonel was separated from his command, and found himself with but two officers and a handful of men. While in this situation, endeavoring to extricate his men from the hosts that pressed them onward, he, scorning to fly, was taken prisoner with his small force of one captain, a lieutenant, and thirty-seven men. The loss of the 69th at Bull Run, in killed, wounded, and prisoners, has been reported at about two hundred.

Corcoran was conveyed to the Libby Prison at Richmond, where for nearly a year he suffered all the indignities and hardships to which Union prisoners were subjected during the war, and for several months was confined with another officer in a damp cellar of the building, having been selected for execution in reprisal for the anticipated punishment of some pirates captured by our seamen. His conduct throughout this trying period was exceedingly manly and dignified; and we have it from an individual, then high in the confidence of the so-called Confederate authorities, that, upon being offered certain privileges, and, in his peculiar position, luxuries, he replied: "I would not take a cup of cold water as a favor from an enemy of the American Union."

In the summer of 1862 he was exchanged, and, coming to New York, was the recipient of many public and private marks of appreciation and esteem. The government commissioned him brigadier-general, and in a short time he raised a brigade of his countrymen, known as the "Corcoran Legion," with which he proceeded to Norfolk, in Virginia. With this body he took part in all General Peck's operations, particularly in the engagement on the river Trent, and the following year was ordered to the Army of the Potomac, with his headquarters at Fairfax Court-House. Some months after, while riding with his staff from Fairfax Station to the Court-House, he was thrown from his horse, and expired four hours afterwards.

His sudden death caused great regret not only to his own friends and countrymen, but among all classes of citizens; for it was felt that the career of a young and promising officer had been too soon brought to a close, and that the country had been deprived of a brave and efficient defender. The loss, indeed, was a national one, for he was an earnest advocate of free government, and an intrepid defender of the American flag.

His Legion survived him, and remained a distinct organization till the close of the war, taking an active and honorable part in the campaigns of 1864-5. Its losses were, of course, very heavy both in men and officers; and among the latter may be mentioned Colonel James McMahon, who fell leading on his men at the battle of Gaines's Mills, Va., June 3d, pierced by fourteen rifle-balls; and General Matthew Murphy, Corcoran's successor, who was mortally wounded in the following campaign. Their blood and that of many another gallant Irishman has moistened and fertilized the sacred soil of Virginia. Let us hope that their noble examples may be as fruitful of high-toned and patriotic actions in those who survive them. There is no class of our people more interested in the stability of this republic, and in the preservation and perpetuation of its fair name and fame, than the adopted citizens of Irish birth; for it has not only been to them a home and a shield of protection against the persecutions of England and the cold scorn of the world, but its influence for good on the destinies of their native country is likely to wax and become more potent as its own strength increases, and its principles of freedom and equality gain acceptance among the nations of Europe. So far we have done well, as have our fathers before us; and it is to be hoped that in the future we will neither throw away the benefits derived from their conduct, nor fail to imitate it should an opportunity present itself.

It would have been a pleasing task for us to have recorded in this volume the names and some of the more prominent achievements of many distinguished Irish officers who shed honor on the country of their birth during the late war for the preservation of the American Union; but their careers are so well known, and their heroism so familiar to us all, that it is unnecessary to allude to them here.

Few citizens, indeed, whether native or foreign, who have not heard of the gallantry of such men as General James Shields of Tyrone, the successful opponent of Stonewall Jackson; Thomas Francis Meagher of Waterford, the principal organizer, and for a long time commander, of the Irish Brigade; Colonels Robert Nugent of Down, and Patrick Kelly of Galway, his successors; General Thomas Smith of Delaware, a native of Cork; Guiney of the 9th Massachusetts Volunteers; Byrne of the 28th Massachusetts Volunteers; St. Clair Mulholland, from the glens of Antrim, of the 116th Pennsylvania Volunteers; O'Kane of the 69th Pennsylvania Volunteers; the devoted Major Joe O'Neill of the 63d, Colonel James Kelly of the 69th New York Volunteers, born in the county of Monaghan; and a host of others of lesser rank, but equally remarkable for devotion to their adopted country, and for unswerving fidelity and undaunted bravery in the darkest hour of our country's tribulations.

Some fell on the field; others have died subsequent to the termination of the war, from the result of physical injuries or over-taxed brain incurred during that dire struggle; and a few yet survive, with undiminished ardor, and with all the unquenchable fire of Irish patriotism burning in their hearts. Future historians and biographers, it is to be hoped, will measure out to them their due meed of justice, which we consider would be unfitting in us to bestow, as well as premature at the present time.

WHO WON THE "BRITISH" VICTORIES?

BATTLES BY LAND AND SEA.

It is humiliating to acknowledge, but it is nevertheless true, that the vast majority of the soldiers and sailors in the English service for several generations past have been natives of Ireland; and it is to them that that country owes the victories, such as those of Nelson and Wellington, Ross, Gough, and Napier, which for the past three-quarters of a century have favored her arms on land and water. During the Peninsular War, two-thirds of the army, according to Lord Edward Bulwer Lytton, were Irish, and in 1810 Sir John Cox Hippesley asserted in his place in Parliament that, among two thousand soldiers, within his own knowledge only one hundred and sixty were Protestants; and in a regiment, then stationed in the south of England, the numbers were even more remarkable, for out of nine hundred men, eight hundred and sixty were Catholics; while the 87th foot, the heroes of Monte Video, were, to a man, of the same faith. In this connection the word "Catholic" is to be taken as synonymous with "Irish," as at that time there were no English and very few Scotch Catholics from whom to recruit.

The same proportion will be found to have existed in the much-lauded British navy. According to Henry Grattan: "In the last war (1775–1782), of eighty thousand seamen, fifty thousand were Irish names; in Chelsea, nearly one-third of the pensioners were Irish names; in some of the men-of-war, nearly the whole complement were Irish." Hippesley on the occasion referred to—and he seems to have given much attention to the matter—affirmed that "when fewer Catholics entered the service than at present, the crew of the *Thunderer*, 74 guns, was composed of two-thirds Catholics."

The same gentleman, himself an orthodox and consistent Protestant, further states that, out of fifty-six ships of the line, which at two different periods belonged to Plymouth division, the Catholics greatly exceeded the Protestants in the majority of the vessels. In some of the first and second rates they formed nearly the whole; and in the Naval Hospital, about four years before, out of four hundred and seventy-six sailors no less than three hundred and sixty-three were Catholics. Alluding to the composition of the British navy in 1782, Sir Jonah Barrington with much justice remarked: "It was then manned by what were generally denominated *British* tars, but a large proportion of whom were in fact sailors of *Irish* birth and *Irish* feelings,—ready to shed their blood in the service of Great Britain whilst she remained the friend of Ireland, but as ready to seize and steer the British navy into Irish ports should she declare against their country. The 'Mutiny of the '*Nore*' confirms these observations. Had the mutineers at that time chosen to carry the

British ships into an Irish port, no power could have prevented them; and had there been a strong insurrection in Ireland, it is more than probable that they would have delivered more than one-half of the English fleet into the hands of their countrymen."

What could and would have been done then, according to Barrington, can be done at any time in the future; and we trust that the day is not far distant when the hardy fellows who have earned so much renown under the enemy's flag, will have one of their own to fight under.

"Hurrah! hurrah! it can't be far when, from the Scinde to Shannon,
Shall gleam a line of freemen's flags, begirt by freemen's cannon,—
The coming day of freedom—the flashing flags of freedom!
      The victor glaive,
      The mottoes wave—
May we be there to read them!—
      That glorious noon,
      God send it soon!
Hurrah for human Freedom!"*

---

* Davis.

www.ingramcontent.com/pod-product-compliance
Lightning Source LLC
Chambersburg PA
CBHW032049220426
43664CB00008B/923